The Art of
Comparative Politics

Ruth Lane
American University

Allyn and Bacon

Boston • London • Toronto • Sydney • Tokyo • Singapore

Vice-President, Editor-in-Chief, Social Sciences: Sean W. Wakely
Senior Editor: Joseph P. Terry
Editorial Assistant: Erika Stuart
Editorial-Production Administrator: Joe Sweeney
Editorial-Production Service: Walsh Associates
Composition Buyer: Linda Cox
Manufacturing Buyer: Suzanne Careau
Cover Administrator: Suzanne Harbison

Library of Congress Cataloging-in-Publication Data

Lane, Ruth, 1935–
    The art of comparative politics / Ruth Lane.
        p.   cm.
    Includes bibliographical references and index.
    ISBN 0–205–26099–3
    1. Comparative government.   I. Title
JF51.L357   1996
320.3—dc20   96–20593
                                                CIP

Printed in United States of America

10 9 8 7 6 5 4 3 2 1   00 99 98 97 96

Contents

Preface

The Art of Comparative Politics is an interpretative essay in the recent history of comparative politics and the present state of its practices, designed to be relevant for anyone, old or young, with an interest in other countries and the ways in which they are studied. The method of the book is selective, focusing on major works in the comparative politics literature and showing what roles they have played in the discipline from its early roots in the behavioral period, to its present emphasis on the new institutional and "state in society" approaches.

The thesis of *The Art of Comparative Politics* is that comparative politics demonstrates not an endless and sometimes incoherent variety of approaches to its subject matters, but a discernible logic of development. If comparative politics has changed its mindset several times over the years, this is interpreted not as aimless wandering but as the necessary steps in a learning process that has led to real progress in the field.

Why the "art" of comparative politics? Students of any field often go to its classics seeking solid, final answers both in terms of substance and method. They wish to know the Euclidean base of assumptions, axioms, postulates, and conclusions upon which they can depend and with the guidance of which they may proceed.

Such absolutes are not possible in comparative politics or in political science generally. I would argue instead that comparativists must learn to fend for themselves, to recognize merit where they find it, but not to assume it is always present; to uncover good ideas even when deeply buried; to beware of errors others may have made. Comparative politics requires, in short, art—the ability to pursue science not under the heavy hand of authority but under the lighter mantle of individual creativity.

The Art of Comparative Politics directs its attention to four periods in the practice of comparative politics. First (Chapter 2), it reevaluates the behavioral movement of the 1960s, seeking to show that the behavioralists were so diverse in their approaches to political science and comparative politics that no one need take up a firm position pro or con behavioralism, but readers can, in practice, use behavioral insights freely to go in many different directions. Thereafter, the essay moves through subsequent phases: the development period (Chapter 3), the return to the state (Chapter 4), and current studies in grassroots and peasant politics, state-in-society, and the new institutionalisms (Chapter 5).

Major attention in each chapter is given not to comprehensive summaries of the different periods, but to selected works that were especially important in the course of the field's development. In the chapter on behavioralism are *The American Voter*, *The Civic Culture*, Downs' theory of democracy, Lipset's political sociology, Dahl's *Who Governs?*, and a sketch of Easton's program.

The development chapter includes Lerner's Turkish village, structural-functionalism, "sequence and crisis" theory and its abrupt end, the work of Huntington and Moore, dependency theory, and Wallerstein's analytic structuralism.

The chapter on the state's being "brought back in" discusses the edited volume by Evans, Rueschemeyer, and Skocpol, with special note of Evans' contribution; Skocpol's *States and Social Revolutions*, O'Donnell's bureaucratic-authoritarian model, and the recent update on political sociology in the European context by Jan-Erik Lane and Svante Ersson; it ends with a brief note on the "deconstruction" of the state.

The final historical chapter reviews the new line of comparative analysis that began with Scott and Popkin's debate over the nature of the peasant, and culminated with Migdal's "melange" model of how the political process itself can become the focus of comparative analysis. Also included are Liebenow's theory of African leadership failures; and in respect to the new institutionalism, works by March and Olsen and Ostrom.

The last chapter presents a variety of theoretic options available to contemporary comparativists, from Michels' iron law, to a new empirical functionalism, to (culturally) rational choice theory. The chapter then goes on, as a summary of the present stage reached by comparativists, to show that the new approaches to grassroots politics, to state-and-society theory, and to institutional analysis are more theoretical than they are sometimes perceived. It suggests that they are similar to modern social science model-building approaches described by Charles Lave and James March.

In choosing to study, in depth, only a sample of the work in comparative politics over recent decades, I do not intend to suggest that only these works were important. But I do seek to show that the selected works effectively represent a "logic" of development in comparative politics, a logic that makes it easier for the reader to place in some coherent framework the specific elements that have woven themselves into the history and the current practice of comparative politics.

Americans tend, perhaps as a byproduct of their long democratic experience, to want inclusiveness—every work that comes to light must be brought in. This is admirable but often loses the forest in its trees. The approach of *The Art of Comparative Politics* is therefore to work for a sharper focus, to delve into detail, and to try to bring clearly into view the contributions, the merits, and especially the interconnectedness of individual works in comparative politics. There is much to be learned from even a checkered past, and those who do not turn to such history are sure to reinvent it.

While the "art" of comparative politics implies that no rock-solid conclusions are to be drawn from the past about contemporary theories or methods, the last chapter suggests that comparative politics' present condition is good, and is a natural culmination of its past, combining a concern both for individuals and for the institutions that create them, even as they are re-creating these institutions. Included in this model are government and politics, functions and structure, people and institutions, ideals and realities—all working to make up a compact and intuitively plausible picture of political action within the broad and challenging context of comparative politics research.

▶ 1

The Science and the Art of Comparative Politics

THE WORLD OF COMPARATIVE POLITICS

Observe a standard chessboard. The pieces are either lined up neatly at the start of a game, or arrayed in orderly confrontation in later stages of the game. Each piece plays its standard part using the rules that govern its moves, in the various situations that arise in the course of the game. The moves and the rules are in a manner of speaking eternal. If your memory capacity is sufficient, there are no surprises in the standard game of chess. It is a mathematically pure realm.

Now imagine a different chessboard, one that tries to maintain its organization in squares but keeps changing shape, from flat plains into mountains and valleys, while new rivers spring up or old ones overflow. The pieces are no longer orderly but dynamic and self-defined: Some may jump off the official playing field into areas they have just discovered or invented. The king may run off with a pawn to seek a new life in another hemisphere; the bishops may enclose a portion of the board and take up sheep farming; the queen's castle and king's knight may stage a coup d'etat; the pawns may rebel and string up their supposed betters. This is not a mathematical realm but something more difficult—a political one.

The "orderly" chess game is a game, designed to provide escape from daily things. The "disorderly" or self-modifying chess game is reality, designed to keep us on our toes if we hope to rise to its many challenges. In the disorderly case the actors are always changing their purposes, always losing and discovering resources, always working within some rules while trying to escape from others. When all else fails, the "pieces" in the disorderly game get together and revolutionize the system itself, rules,

1

resources, mountains, and rivers altogether. In this real world, creativity and stupidity are equally evident, and everyone plays his or her own game with all the rules open to modification, either for good or ill. This dynamic reality is the home of comparative politics.

What is comparative politics? It is two things, first a world, second a discipline. As a "world," comparative politics encompasses political behavior and institutions in all parts of the earth, in Africa, Asia, Europe, Latin America, as well as North America. The "world" of comparative politics includes the collapse of the Soviet Union, and the rise of the European Union; includes economic growth in East Asia, and economic stagnation in many parts of Africa; includes war in the former Yugoslavia, and the beginnings of peace in the Middle East; includes democratization in Latin America and militarization in Southeast Asia; includes hope and despair, failure and success, mixed everywhere together in what we know as the contemporary political world.

The "discipline" of comparative politics is a field of study that desperately tries to keep up with, to encompass, to understand, to explain, and perhaps to influence the fascinating and often riotous world of comparative politics. Comparative politics as an area of study goes back to Greek antiquity, and has continued sporadically throughout history, but has achieved a special importance at the close of the twentieth century, when economics, technology, travel, and communications have brought all areas of the world into deep interdependence. Faraway countries are no longer far away; differences of culture can no longer be ignored; the cheerful hope that economic development will occur painlessly has long since faded away; and the desperate hope that national self-interests can be kept under peaceful control seems of questionable validity. The social sciences might be expected to be of assistance in such a period, but rarely fulfill that promise.

Comparative politics is unusual among the social sciences in the degree to which its progress has been driven by a confrontation with hard facts, indeed, recalcitrant facts. Many social science theories survive largely because they cannot be tested; but in comparative politics there are test situations in every direction one looks, and across every border one steps. It is perhaps for this reason that modern comparative politics has, since the 1950s, made real progress in both theory and research. The present work seeks to chart some aspects of that progress.

The study of comparative politics, like the study of the other sciences, has had a logic of its own, a developmental pattern that combined specific questions about the various nations and peoples in the world, specific data, and specific problems, all within a learning process that has taken a specific direction and reached a working synthesis of its own past. One interesting aspect of this developmental process within comparative politics is that it has not always followed the various maps set out for it, but has taken its own course, has been to a large degree self-organizing. Comparative politics, in other words, has learned from its own practical experiences in the field, experiences strongly shaped by the need to cope with the facts of daily political life in an array of very diverse societies.

Comparative politics, as an object of study, often presents serious difficulties to its students (and its teachers) because of the conceptual level it must seek to achieve in order to fulfill its purpose of acquiring an understanding of diverse societies. Human beings are not usually born with an innate talent for theoretical thinking, which requires high levels of abstraction combined with a concrete grasp of interesting practical facts. Yet because of the importance, in an increasingly multicultural world, of the subject areas covered by comparative politics, it is desirable for those who have such interests to acquire a better sense of theory, its goals and its practices, and its hazards. One way to achieve conceptual skills is to watch experts in a given field as they struggle, over time, to develop their science.

This book traces out a logic of the recent history of comparative politics by studying a selection of comparative works, classics either in themselves or in relation to the development of the field, that are grouped in four basic periods: behavioralism, development theory, the return to the state, and the discovery of analytic institutionalism, the individual political actor embedded in surrounding social institutions. Rather than attempting comprehensive coverage of every tree in the comparative politics forest, this classics approach focuses on those major writings that served at various periods to exert independent force in defining the comparative field. The selection of scholars has been kept reasonably small in order to facilitate an overall understanding of where modern comparative politics started, what paths it took and what roadblocks it encountered, what it learned along the way, and where it finds itself in the present. As an analysis this essay does not claim to be decisive, but to suggest a coherent interpretation of the comparative politics field, with the hope that it might stimulate other such efforts, and might be useful in defining future research.

A major thesis of the present work is that comparative politics has in recent decades indeed defined for itself a real and fruitful direction. Starting from the behavioral period, which comparativists have never fully accepted but from which they can never quite escape; through the development-dependency period with all its conflicts and disillusionments; and into the study of the dissolving monolith of the state, comparative politics today shows signs of settling on a viable research model, that of the individual actor embedded in social institutions and acting strategically within that political basis. While not as yet fully defined, this approach emphasizes a microanalytic approach to political behavior, centering on real people, not grand abstractions, on the individuals' surrounding social, political, and economic constraints, and on the sometimes creative activity of individuals to avoid, avert, outdistance, or overthrow their institutions. This new model does not by any means solve all the problems of comparative politics, but it opens up specific questions and routes of research, which are perhaps more interesting than final answers would be.

Comparative politics is a constantly evolving discipline, taking more seriously than some other subfields within political science the scientific mandate to combine theory and facts into a scientific synthesis that will make itself useful in a complex world. The better we understand the history of this quest, the more likely it is that we can contribute to its future.

COMPARATIVE POLITICS AS PRACTICE

The study of comparative politics is particularly appropriate today because it is the study of what we see all around us—the differences in social behavior among people of different cultures, nations, and places. Comparative politics begins where many inquiries stop: with the richness and diversity of human experience, experience that ranges from everyday customs to the deep-seated notions of how the world should be organized—those ideas that we sometimes call justice. Because the study of these human differences extends even to the different ways different people think—the ways they cognitively organize their lives—comparative politics may even be seen as an adjunct of philosophy. The old philosophers sought the meaning of truth; the new comparative politics seeks to understand what different kinds of people define as truth and how that definition influences their lives and interactions with one another. This does not necessarily mean, it should be noted, that there are no universal truths; but it is something that can no longer be taken for granted, and must be subjected to empirical tests.

Comparative political science starts us down this road. It is concerned with trying to understand people from "the other side of the globe," whichever side you happen to be on. But it is equally concerned with understanding neighbors, peoples who live next door but whom one has never gotten to know well enough to understand them in their own terms. Comparative politics in its most general sense is the essence of political science, because comparative politics forces its students to do what all political scientists should do but often do not, to "compare" people and political institutions with an open mind, and to appreciate the relativity of human ways and institutions. If the customs of people in other lands seem alien, comparative politics teaches us to bear in mind that "they" also think "we" are barbarians, "foreigners." The first lesson of comparative politics is that, very often, nobody admires anyone but him- or herself. Remembering this rule "puts us in our place" and allows inquiry to begin with an open mind. If later on, evaluations of different customs and institutions are to be made, much study is necessary before one is entitled to make judgments on which forms of government are desirable, and for whom.

All this is quite different from "multiculturalism" or "political correctness," both of which generally involve adopting determinedly favorable attitudes to people different from oneself, or at least of being very careful not to offend people even though one may think their ways of life are quite dreadful. Whatever one thinks of this approach, it is not science but an ethical program. Science is concerned not with telling people how to run their lives but with studying and comprehending facts. A comparative politics that aspires to be a science is concerned with understanding people, not with judging them. Comparative politics may hope to be relevant to how we feel about other people, but those feelings are not a proper part of comparative politics. Complete neutrality may be beyond the strength of most human beings, but the study of comparative politics at least asks us to make the effort to be objective.

To advocate the "art" of comparative politics many seem inconsistent, for it is a major theme of the present work that political science can be a science, and that comparative politics will continue to play a major role in developing such a science. Any inconsistency between the two terms is however only superficial, stemming from a very narrow interpretation of both the terms science and art. If art is putting oil on canvas in ways intended to be aesthetically interesting, and if science is test tubes and cyclotrons, then art and science are indeed two very different occupations. But if art is seen as the creative approach to reality, and science is seen as the discipline of inquiry into the real world, then the distinction disappears and art becomes an integral part of science.

"COMPARED TO WHAT?"

Comparative politics is a difficult business. All science is, of course, difficult, but comparative politics is difficult in a deeper way. The physical sciences as we encounter them in school are all well developed. The physicists, chemists, biologists of the past set their sciences on their proper course, decades or even centuries ago, by defining basic approaches, concepts, and methods. Finding the appropriate conceptual frameworks is not easy. Apples had been falling on people's heads for years before Newton took the event seriously enough to begin the systematic inquiry into gravity. The chemical elements had existed since about the time of creation, but were only ordered into the periodic table by Mendeleyev in the nineteenth century. The study of social and political institutions has proceeded more slowly, since while physical phenomena have a regularity and stability that invites scientific inquiry, social phenomena are harder to get a grip on. Perhaps more important, in the physical sciences explanations can be falsified more promptly. People can put your ideas into their own test tubes and it may often happen that your results do not happen as predicted.

In the social sciences, however, it is different. So many complex factors are involved in every human event, and it is so difficult to focus inquiry only on specific concepts, that weak explanations or theories are hard to disprove and last longer than they ought. If you think a rain dance will bring rain, and yet rain does not occur after the dance is celebrated, then the "theorist" can always argue, "you didn't do the dance right." Since bad theories are hard to recognize, it is often true that *good* theories are not given the preference they deserve but are lumped promiscuously with approaches that lack either clarity or rigor.

Theories—defined roughly as statements that order, define, and explain the real world—are important because they identify for us what concepts are to be seen as relevant, how the concepts are related, and what processes are at work in whatever it is that we are studying. Good theories are more than important, they are vital to scientific life itself because they give guidance about what are the best concepts, interactions, and processes to study. A bad theory, conversely, can lead investigators widely astray, sometimes for generations.

Tradition has it that once, when Socrates was asked "How's your wife?", he responded "Compared to what?" This exchange has frequently been interpreted as a commentary on Socrates' marriage. But the question is relevant here because it captures in a nutshell the central problem of comparative politics. The French and the English are different . . . "Compared to what?" The Chinese and the Indians are different . . . "Compared to what?" The Venezuelans and the Uruguayans are different . . . "Compared to what?" The Hausa and the Igbo. . . . "Compared to what?"

Tourists and travelers, challenged to say exactly what is different about the nations they have visited, will pick superficial comparisons—what the people eat, how they dress, whether their streets are safe to walk after dark. Media reports are similarly superficial, as commentators select out such momentous events as the Russians' newly discovered enthusiasm for baseball! Even where serious events are reported, the discussion stays firmly on the surface; faced with a civil war somewhere, the emphasis is on "Who is winning?" or "Are Americans in danger?" or "Do civilians need aid?" Very rarely does anyone ask why they are fighting in the first place. Perhaps we assume we already know the answer: The parties are fighting because they are different. And it always therefore comes back to Socrates' question, different "compared to what?"

Faced with this problem, in the past many comparativists have adopted a practice that seems obvious, and yet is vigorously and terribly wrong. They have said in essence, "compared to us." All the diversity of culture, history, and experience has thus been obliterated by the dumb question, How do these people stack up against ourselves—against the most progressive, enlightened, virtuous, indeed most lovable people in the world? This is such a blockheaded approach that once recognized it collapses of its own absurdity. But it has not always been recognized.

THE NEED FOR BASIC PRINCIPLES

What then is the proper way to compare different groups or nations or cultures? That is what we do not know. Comparative politics to date is the history of the search. Ideally, comparative political scientists would have a general outline of "things that are important in defining a political society." They could then begin their study of a given society with the guidance of this general outline. It would tell them what aspects of the society they should study in order to understand how it works, how its various practices fit together, what principles are involved in its operation. Then when some passerby asks, "How's Bangladesh?", one would not have to wonder "compared to what" but would have real theory to work with in explaining how the Bangladeshi system works.

If the theory were a satisfactory one, such explanations might be reasonably compact. One would not have to say "to fully understand the English one must look at their history since 1066," and go on to fill this out in ten or more bulky volumes. Instead one could say, "English society at present operates according to several basic principles, which manifest themselves in all major institutional areas," and then summarize these principles. This may sound like an unrealistically rigorous goal, yet one must note that physical scientists do it all the time. To understand why eggshells dissolve in lemon juice you need not have a history of the egg or the lemon, but need only the relevant properties of each.

Critics greet such a claim with the argument that human societies are far more complex than the physical world. This argument may have a whiff of truth in it, but it is based largely on the misapprehension common to nonscientists of thinking the physical world is "easy" to understand. Pick up any physics textbook and it will cure this delusion. Everything, physical and social alike, is complicated. The difference between the physical and the social sciences is largely one of courage. Faced with unknown territory, physical scientists rush out to investigate it. Social scientists, on the other hand, are likely to sit on the frontier fence and admire the difficulties.

The search for theoretically useful conceptual structures is long but not without discoveries, although whatever is found is but a stage in the further inquiry. It is possible today to argue that comparative politics has reached a plateau in its search. After decades, or centuries if one wants to extend the history back to its founding fathers, comparative politics may have achieved the kind of microanalytic basis that Democritus bestowed on physics in the beginning period of that science.

To affirm that societies, political systems, and institutions are at bottom composed of human individuals does not seem difficult. However, comparativists had first to wrestle with other approaches, looking at societies as wholes, before it was concluded that political systems do not exist in abstract grandeur but are made up of people who vote, people who are voted for, people who claim expertise for certain roles, and so on; and that societies work in certain ways because young individuals are taught by older individuals to follow certain rules and practices. These common patterns are called institutions, and the current focus in comparative politics is on individual persons as created by, yet constantly recreating, their institutions.

Institutions that have seemed in the past to be more powerful and more enduring than individuals are now often recognized to be only as strong as the beliefs individual people have in the institutions' rightness. If the collapse of the USSR taught us nothing else, it did make a vivid illustration of the truth that even apparently monolithic institutions may dissolve like the mountain mists. It should give all political scientists, including students of comparative politics, cause for thought.

How does the student of comparative politics analyze whole societies from an individual or microanalytic level? The first step is to understand that societies, polities, and their institutions must, if they are to exist, be operative principles in the minds of real men and women. The Pentagon building, set like a monument overlooking the Potomac, has no independent existence as an institution apart from (1) the people who work there and believe they have the right or the ability to make certain decisions for the American republic, and (2) the people who don't work there but who also think the people who do work there have certain rights. Without the people we could paint the Pentagon pink and convert it to a shopping mall. Without people and their beliefs, values, and institutional roles, buildings have no meaning. Buildings are not institutions but only means of keeping the rain off the heads of the people who are the real institutions.

THE "SOCIAL" NATURE OF REALITY

To understand human behavior as both individual and institutional, as the student of comparative politics must do in order to study whole societies without getting misled by abstractions, a brief consultation with the social psychologists is helpful. A classic text dealing with the issues of institution formation is the book with the almost humorous title, *The Social Construction of Reality,* by Peter Berger and Thomas Luckmann (1967). They are not however joking. Their point is exactly that "reality," that is, what we all think of as reality, is created in the course of human interactions. "Surely not!" one may protest; "if I drive my automobile directly at that tree at 50 MPH, a *real* reality will result, and I will be *really,* not socially, injured." True, but hear them out before deciding if this is the norm.

Berger and Luckmann begin with the idea long since noticed by social philosophers such as Montesquieu and Rousseau that human beings are distinguished from others in the animal world by their learning flexibility. Where birds and animals are from birth programmed by their genetic composition to behave in particular ways, human beings require a long period of learning before they are able to make their way in the world. It is during this long period of learning that human beings become "institutionalized."

The meaning of the term institution as Berger and Luckmann use it is wider than the definitions we commonly use, which very often imply large complex sociopolitical structures operating within four walls, such as educational institutions, penal institutions, or mental institutions. Other everyday definitions of institutions emphasize that an institution is a formal or "official" grouping of people, such as the U.S. Congress, the welfare department, or the sheriff's office.

Berger and Luckmann enlarge these ideas. For them an institution is any patterned human interaction combining mutual expectations in respect to the behavior of the participants. So, if you have been hiring someone to mow your lawn all summer, and if you expect him to turn up at regular intervals, and he expects you to pay promptly with a check that does not bounce; and if he does in fact turn up regularly to mow the lawn; and you do properly pay, then you two have an informal but real institutional bond. And if the mower decides he should be paid more, or you decide he should mow more often, then you both negotiate and modify the institution. "Negotiation" is, of course, only an abstract term to describe much more intuitive behavior. He may look cross every time he comes by, and you may begin to wonder if you are paying enough; you offer more money, he snaps it up and henceforth looks more cheerful. The result is that the institution has been changed: Not all the rules have been changed, but some are different. Thus, institutions have continuity but are not necessarily rigid.

Now if that kind of very immediate behavior is seen as within the idea of institutionalization, it becomes clearer how Berger and Luckmann can say we are institutional creatures. Since learning is the process that teaches us our roles in institutions, the question becomes who does the teaching. Berger and Luckmann stay at a very local level in order to make their point clear, and their answer to "who teaches?" is that the people who get there first teach those who come after. Usually this means the elder teach the younger, and in Berger and Luckmann's example the lessons may be quite arbitrary.

If the "society" into which a person is born consists of three people, each of whom has different habits, tastes, and values, then the "truths" that are passed on to the new member will not be truths at all but will reflect the various compromises the three people have made in order to live conveniently together. Rules that were originally made merely to suit the proclivities of the first generation (Peter will hunt game, Paul will plant potatoes) may become for succeeding generations absolute mandates: this "kind" of person does this "kind" of work. When children consent to these pre-existing principles, institutions continue; when children do not consent, institutions are revised or overthrown.

TO WHAT EXTENT IS BEHAVIOR INSTITUTIONALLY DEFINED?

Most people tend to think of their own actions as personally motivated, if those actions are not overtly or directly coerced; that is, unless some other person is visibly forcing us to do something, we assume our action is freely taken. What is less obvious is the type of action that is neither quite free nor quite forced, that is, "institutional" behavior that we have internalized. It is this institutionalized range of behavior that embeds individuals in groups and nations, embeds them in the different groups that are the source of that type of behavior. It is vital to the study of comparative politics to realize how very comprehensive is this type of institutionalized behavior, because it is through institutionalized behavior that social scientists are able to summarize and study the behavior of national and other social groups.

As a homely example, take an action as mundane and apparently personal as your brushing your teeth. Surely this cannot be anything but private choice? In fact, it is totally institutional. First of all, your parents taught you to do it, giving plausible reasons such as that having healthy clean teeth is a desirable goal whereas decay and toothaches are unpleasant. That is one institutional level; but where did your parents get the idea they pass on to you? The second institutional source is the medical profession, the members of which agree on a more or less standardized set of precepts for their patients, and every time you visit a dentist these precepts are "imposed" upon you.

But notice that not every group in society takes good care of its health, and if you do so you mark yourself as a member of a third institutional group, a social class that has time and money to worry about dental hygiene. Fourth, the medical profession and social classes are both influenced by the larger surrounding culture, and their advice and customs as transmitted to individuals are marked by membership in cultural institutions. If asked why one brushes one's teeth one gives various "rational" reasons for doing so, but the real reason is that "people like myself tend to do it." In other words, the behavior is institutionalized.

That behavior is institutional does not preclude its being rational—brushing does decrease decay—but what is considered rational changes over time. It also changes in different societies: Eating a healthy diet with no refined sugars, for instance, is also a way to have healthy teeth, but is not a solution the modern American usually finds compatible with his or her institutionalized tastes. So if you did brush your teeth this morning, it was not a personal act but one that marked you as a person of a particular time, particular group, particular class, and so on. And if such an apparently personal kind of behavior is actually not personal but institutional, then even more must it be said that more interesting human behavior is institutional—including the norms suggested by religion, ethnic identity, class, gender, or occupation.

INSTITUTIONAL ALTERNATIVES AND CHANGE

The main point remains both simple and important: a very large percentage of each human individual's behavior is institutionally based. Each individual is like the center of a series of nested boxes, each of which guides her or his behavior in the various circumstances in which each is located. Sometimes the boxes are not nested but competing, and where this is the case the individual must make choices between the alternatives offered by different institutions. But notice that even the alternatives are controlled by institutions. Mary may choose not to go to law school, as her parents had hoped; and instead chooses to become a musician, as her friends have urged. But until very recently neither her parents nor her friends suggested she might become an electrical engineer; This was an alternative that did not exist in the options available to women until someone made an issue of it. So influences trickle down from higher level institutions to lower level ones, and influences bubble up from lower level institutions to higher level ones. To study institutions, therefore, the comparativist must focus on the nuts and bolts of individual actions, hopes, fears, and expectations; for that is where institutions manifest themselves.

THE PRACTICE OF COMPARATIVE POLITICS

The model of individuals created by their institutions and yet continually recreating those institutions is an important one for modern comparative politics because it allows the researcher to grasp the operation of whole societies without losing the concrete basis upon which theories become testable. In the past, comparativists have tried to develop theories of sufficient generality so that all countries and cultures might be subsumed under them. While the intention was good because it was an attempt to follow, in comparative politics, positivist standards for scientific research, the result of these abstractions tended to be unsatisfactory because they did not lead to the vigorous testing and evaluation necessary if science is to separate good from bad theories. But the microinstitutional model currently popular in comparative politics research is closely tied to observable behavior, both at the grassroots citizen level and at the elite political level.

If comparativists have reached some consensus on the model of microinstitutionalism, then why not simply go out and practice comparative politics without studying its past at all? The reason is that knowledge of the past is necessary in order to be able intelligently to practice comparative politics in the present. As is said of history, those who do not study comparative politics are condemned to repeat it. For comparative politics, as for all new sciences, the history of the discipline educates its students not only into the causes of practices that must at least occasionally seem to be "damn-foolishness," it also reminds students of the good ideas that do not deserve to be thrown out with the rest of the bathwater. Moreover, the history of comparative politics offers many enduring ideas, concerns, and problems with which the current comparativist needs to be acquainted.

Some day it would be desirable to understand the range of political systems, cultures, and alternative options sufficiently well to be of some use to nations or peoples who themselves come looking for help. Giving advice without being asked is the last form of colonialism and is properly looked upon with disapproval. But suppose a beleaguered leader from some distant country, or even perhaps from your own country, took the "political science" label on comparative politics seriously and asked your advice about some severe problem. What if Gorbachev had come by? What if the Nigerians turn up? What if Vermont really wants to secede? The possibilities should give considerable food for thought about our comparativist responsibilities.

In the practice of comparative politics, research and theory are equally important, and should always be combined: Actual research must parallel the study of concepts and theories; and the study of theories must proceed in the context of actual research problems. Every abstract idea needs to be applied rigorously to real situations in real countries, and every country should be studied with abstract ideas in mind. Too much emphasis is often given in comparative politics to the sometimes mindless comparison of at least two countries, so that the "comparative" mandate is mechanically fulfilled. But often we do not know enough at the start to know which countries are suitable for comparison.

The use of conceptual frameworks that broaden the student's perspective on any individual country being investigated is what raises the study to a comparative level, not merely the rote comparison of "in Brazil they do it this way, in Argentina, that way." Such an approach will be sterile unless combined with conceptual intelligence. It is important to realize constantly that comparison is a means, not an end. The end or purpose is the understanding of different systems and societies in rich, rigorous, scientific form. But nothing so completely shows us how little we know as the attempt to compare. So if comparison is only a means, it is a very important means both for the generation, testing, and evaluation of theories, and for keeping our noses ever closer to the scientific grindstone.

HOW TO GET STARTED

Comparative politics can seem to be a difficult topic, especially for beginners, because it abounds with conceptual structures bearing opaque names such as "political sociology" or "structural-functionalism"; and the student despairs of keeping everything straight, of figuring out where to classify the various writers. The best antidote to such problems is to renounce the idea that comparative politics is an orderly, timeless conceptual whole, and to accept the common sense notion that comparative politics, like everything else, developed over time in a kind of dialectical challenge and response. One author developed a theoretical idea, others criticized it, or perhaps events undermined some of its main precepts, and the original idea turned into a modified form of itself, or if the critics were very vociferous, turned into its apparent opposite.

Thomas Kuhn (1962) has argued that all science is thus, that certain clusters of ideas and practices called paradigms exist in the scientific community only until they are replaced, after a political battle, with a more acceptable paradigm. Some political scientists have accepted this argument at the philosophical level as an escape from constricting rules of scientific procedure, but surprisingly few have actually applied the approach to their own history. Instead of accepting the push and pull of revolutionaries against the status quo, as vividly defined by Kuhn, there is often a tendency to try to fit everyone into a single smooth curve of history. This is a misleading picture for new students of the comparative field, because it suggests a degree of organization that never existed. Kuhn's more realistic image suggests that science is an ongoing battle, based on sharp differences and odd alliances. This political process is unified only across time, as ideas sort themselves out through active conflict. To understand comparative politics, in this view, the student must study the intellectual arguments of which it has been composed. This is the approach taken here.

GENERAL ORGANIZATION OF THE BOOK

The present analysis of the recent history of comparative politics divides it into four major periods, each sharing common themes within its diversity. The first of these periods, discussed in Chapter 2, went under the militant name of the Behavioral Revolution, and, however people felt about the prospect of making comparative politics a "real science," the behavioral era made a permanent impression on all the fields within political science. Behavioralists presented a methodological argument that emphasized above all things the collection of numerical data on actual human political behavior, and the organization of these data into correlational patterns that would allow political scientists to predict political outcomes. Even in the 1990s the student of comparative politics can hear behavioral themes in current debates, as scholars argue over theories, criticize one another for methodological failures, and seek to justify their conclusions on grounds of the data upon which those conclusions were based.

The second period that defined itself within comparative politics, the subject of Chapter 3, was the development movement that grew parallel with behavioralism; this period was by far the more coherent of the two movements, and was far less quantitative in its commitment. The topic of development, as is often the case in science and scholarship, was forced on comparative politics by current events, here the political changes of the years after the Second World War, when new nations offered challenge and hope to a whole generation of comparativists. In an attempt to bring all different types of societies, old and new, under a single common umbrella, development theorists centered their attention on the highest conceptual levels, expanding their science's scope to societies and economies as well as political systems. The period was marked by exceptional progress in many areas of comparative politics, yet in the course of time the original optimism sank into disillusionment because of the widespread failures of both societies and theories.

This situation led, in the mid-1970s, to a collective reassertion of tradition, but tradition in a new form shaped by behavioralism and developmentalism, as comparativists reasserted the importance of political institutions and launched the third of the four major movements within the discipline, the "bringing back in" of the state. This is the subject area covered by Chapter 4. Where earlier periods had sent comparative politics students out among sociologists, anthropologists, and economists in the search for advice, the state-centered approach sent scholars back to European sources in political economy and political sociology, taking from these writings the important conclusion that governments were of vital importance in national development. State theorists also found that the state could sometimes be very weak and very strong simultaneously; and that it was difficult to generalize about "the state" at all, because it was made up of so many different actual people and agencies with so many different agendas and opportunities, all acting in disparate ways.

This "dissolution" of the state led directly, in the late 1980s and early 1990s to the two strands that together mark the last of the four periods here defined, which is discussed in Chapter 5. In this latest stage, inquiry is directed towards concrete individuals who make choices and carry out actions in specific institutional contexts, and who may, if the occasion arises, change the formal and informal institutions within which they live their political lives. The latest stage has encompassed in a novel way many of the concerns of earlier periods: the individualism and attention to data of the behavioralists; the concern with social organization and change of the developmentalists; and the emphasis on the role of institutions of the state theorists.

The latest stage can also be defined as one of disillusionment with the earlier three stages: disillusion with the behavioralists' reductionism, lack of context and shallowness of explanation; disillusion with the developmentalists' idealism, abstraction, and ambiguity; disillusion with the statists' assumption that "the" state existed and that it could or should be strong. That combination of lessons learned from the past and disillusions with the past form the logic of comparative politics as it is traced here.

THE MIXED BEHAVIORAL REVOLUTION

The behavioral period that is the subject of Chapter 2 was wider than comparative politics proper, although it contained comparative works of major importance; and this wider context, because it provided a background to events in comparative politics then and now, is important to understanding its history. The chapter begins with Roy Macridis' (1955) complaint against the "traditionalists" of the past, a complaint representative of what others in other fields were expressing, that the old timers had been parochial, impractical, unsystematic, and inattentive to real-world politics. Like other behavioralists' complaints, Macridis' criticisms of the past were vigorous without as yet providing much guidance on what the up-to-date critic should do to improve upon the past.

The behavioralist shot heard round the discipline, which provided a methodological model for the discipline for many years, was *The American Voter* (Campbell, Converse, Miller, and Stokes, 1960), included in Chapter 2 because of its strong research influence on all fields of political science, including comparative politics. Surveys were a two-edged sword. On the one hand, they taught political scientists more facts than they had ever wanted to know about citizens' indifference to politics. In addition to this unhappy lesson, survey techniques had a methodological mandate as well, that henceforth political scientists, including comparativists, must add courses in methodology and statistical techniques to their repertoires. Shock waves from this campaign are still regularly observed in contemporary political science and comparative politics.

The survey-oriented approach was brought particularly home to students of comparative politics in *The Civic Culture* (Almond and Verba, 1963), which studied civic attitudes in Germany, Britain, Italy, Mexico, and the United States. Chapter 2 argues that this five-nation study had a wide impact in comparative politics, an impact that was both positive and negative. The new techniques were put in service of some very traditional issues of citizenship behavior, and the results cleared away many illusions about the nature of democratic culture; all this was positive for further research. On the other hand, more negatively, the technical virtuosity of the book set a discouragingly high standard for others to emulate, and nurtured a latent hostility in the discipline to large-scale behavioralist research.

Because Chapter 2 seeks to provide a realistic background to behavioralism's impact on comparative politics, it emphasizes the lack of coherence in the actual behavioralist movement and includes works that were important in their influence but led in all possible directions, not easily subsumed under any neat definition. Anthony Downs' *Economic Theory of Democracy* (1957), for instance, would come to be part of an ideal model against which theories in comparative politics would be judged in later years, yet was thoroughly different in method and style from the survey-based approaches. By taking a simplified model of a political system and evaluating rational choice by leaders and citizens within that model, Downs showed the serious intellectual problems inherent in democratic government, and sharpened the discipline's appreciation of logical analysis. These seeds would not flourish in comparative politics until the fourth period defined above, based on the individual-in-institutions model.

Another example in Chapter 2 of the diversity in behavioralism as it affected comparative politics was Seymour Martin Lipset's *Political Man* (1959), which used the traditions of class analysis to investigate the society-wide conditions of democratic government, in the search both for democracy and stability. This approach was rich in data, yet data of a type different from that provided by survey research; again illustrating how false it is to overstate the unity of behavioralism. A work of similarly high status in the behavioral canon, yet equally unclassifiable, was Robert Dahl's *Who Governs?* (1961), a data-rich study of local government behavior, centered on the different patterns of government and the different social groups that supported them. The analysis emphasizes how diverse were Dahl's tools and commitments, and how difficult it was to distill from this famous work any useful guidelines for political research generally.

Chapter 2, having tried by illustration to show how rich a brew behavioralism was, containing everything from survey research to aggregate statistics, from deductive economics to case-oriented sociology, concludes with David Easton's "behavioral creed," suggesting that this image of behavioralism was not entirely in accord with its actuality, as shown in the work of Campbell et al., Lipset, Almond and Verba, Downs, and Dahl; and that behavioralism is not a unified approach to be rejected as too strict for comparative politics research, but a goldmine of possibilities.

THE DEVELOPMENT PERIOD

Against the diverse background of behavioralism in political science, and comparative politics' specific role in that movement, research in the field took its primary direction under the guidance of development, the topic of the second major period into which comparative politics has been classified here. Chapter 3 looks back at the early years of development theory from a position later in history, when hard lessons had been forced upon investigators about the political, social, and economic obstacles facing development. Because it is difficult today for students to appreciate in retrospect what the world looked like to comparativists of the time, the discussion of the development period begins with a tale from Daniel Lerner's *The Passing of Tradi-*

tional Society (1958) recounting how the Turkish village of Balgat went from being dusty, isolated, poor, and stagnant, to achieving new roads, new transportation, electricity, and wells, all as the result of the democratic political process. For a while it seemed blessedly simple, as indeed it may seem to students today who enter the field for the first time.

Another example in Chapter 3 of this early optimism was the book that gave the new field its name, Gabriel Almond's and James Coleman's *The Politics of the Developing Areas* (1960), where the hopeful future connotations of "development" replaced the pessimistic connotations of "tradition," a term marked for modern scholars with associations of a dead hopeless past. One aspect of the Almond and Coleman book was simply to introduce the underdeveloped world to comparativists who previously had looked only on the major European states as their proper purview. But Chapter 3's analysis emphasizes the major contribution of the book as the introduction of comparative politics' first major attempt at theory building in the new international world, the theory called, as was the sociological theory that inspired it, structural-functionalism. Because the theory postulated that in every society, no matter how distant, certain functions (needs) had to be fulfilled, this functional theory promised to be truly comparative, bringing all countries under a single conceptual apparatus.

Chapter 3 includes other approaches to development, many of which made independent theoretical contributions, although not always recognized at the time. One of the classics of the early development period was Samuel Huntington's *Political Order in Changing Societies* (1968), an iconoclastic series of studies that emphasized the difficulties faced by new societies not only in creating economic progress but merely in maintaining a modicum of social order, given the various warring groups in what Huntington called "praetorian" societies. Huntington was unique in suggesting that politics, not economics, was the key to development; in being willing to entertain harsh government methods to ensure order; and in arguing that the United States was not a good model for new states to follow because its whole history was an anomaly in Western political development, a kind of Tudor hangover.

Another major work of the period discussed in Chapter 3 was Barrington Moore's *Social Origins of Dictatorship and Democracy* (1966), which sought through the comparative historical analysis of many nations to determine the causal factors that led to national political outcomes, specifically to fascism, democracy, and communism. Moore's emphasis was on economic class analysis, and continued to bear analytic fruit well into later periods of the comparative politics literature.

The development school as a whole presents a major example of the ability of comparativists to learn from practical experience and intellectual criticism, because of its response to an important group of theorists who vehemently challenged its premises, its assumptions, and its practices—the "dependency" critics. This "correction" was brought about largely by theorists from Latin America who spoke, in the name of the entire underdeveloped world, for a perspective that saw development not as the benign care of the rich for their poorer relatives, but as capitalist exploitation that put the rest of the world into a state of underdevelopment and dependency, and kept it there. Chapter 3 analyzes Cardoso and Faletto's *Dependency and Development in Latin America* (1979) as illustrative of this argument. The claim that imperialism had disguised itself as development theory resonated in circles both inside and outside the scholarly community.

The dependency critique, along with internal criticism from developmentalists themselves, caused a rethinking of existing development theory; the depressing state of actual Third World nations, racked by poverty and tyranny, added to the decline of functional development approaches. In the vacuum that followed, particular attention settled on an outgrowth of the dependency movement, the world systems theory represented in the conclusion of Chapter 3 by Immanuel Wallerstein's *The Modern World System* (1974), with its conceptual emphasis on "core" and "periphery" and the uneven relationship between them. The chapter's analysis argues that Wallerstein's richly historical analytic approach is not merely a theory of inter-nation behavior, but has major relevance to comparative politics in its detailed picture of how in history various nations flourished or declined, in part as a result of world conditions but also in part because of the domestic forces of society and politics.

BACK TO THE STATE

In Chapter 4 the third stage in recent comparative research history brings the observer to the movement colloquially known as "bringing the state back in," or, in other words, the first re-examination of the state since the behavioral revolution had cast it into the oblivion of being old-fashioned. The return to the state began with an attempt to develop theory about the state as a whole, as illustrated in the theoretic chapters of the book that gave the movement its name (Evans, Rueschmeyer, and Skocpol, 1985), and Chapter 4 opens with these discussions. It was notable however that even in the early days, researchers discovered that "the state" did not exist, was instead a complex combination of different persons and groups with interesting connections to other parts of the societies in question. In one well-known study, Evans (1987) showed how the dependency relationship presupposed by the dependencistas turned out in reality to be a far more complex situation, a tangled mix of state officials engaged in often successful strategic negotiation with their supposed exploiters.

Also included in Chapter 4 is an analysis of Theda Skocpol's influential *States and Social Revolutions* (1979), a book that directly attacked the functionalist perspective, arguing instead that economic (structural) factors were the major influence in history, and that ideas and volitions were largely irrelevant to social progress. Skocpol's analysis of the French and Russian Revolutions revealed unexpected similarities of bureaucratic organization between the two, unlike the English revolutionary model; and in a fine chapter on the long Chinese revolution, Skocpol analyzed those revolutionary years from a structural perspective that was as much political as economic.

The re-emphasis on the state also served an integrating function in comparative politics, bringing into the dialogue earlier works that had fallen outside the functionalist development paradigm, such as Guillermo O'Donnell's analysis of the bureaucratic authoritarian experience in Latin America (1988) . Chapter 4 argues that like other state theorists, O'Donnell's strength was in the method he employed of decomposing the elements of society and state into social, economic, and political groups; of analyzing. their expectations about one another's behavior, and of showing how the complex interactive process could result in socioeconomic breakdown, with authoritarian rule the final result. The thrust of this analysis was an important force in educating developmentalists in the possibility that economic development might have serious negative outcomes; but the method itself deserved attention for its down-to-earth strategy of integrating disparate elements in a coherent, political model of explanation.

Finally, Chapter 4 takes up another dimension of state analysis, the synthesizing overview by Jan-Erik Lane and Svante Ersson (1991) based on a re-evaluation of the political sociology tradition in the context of its utility as a full theory of the state. *Politics and Society in Western Europe* picked its way carefully through the basic assumptions about democracy and stability characteristic of the political sociology approach, and subjected each to rigorous comparison with data from throughout the European experience. This was behavioralism harnessed to the statist inquiry, and the result showed serious weaknesses in Western political scientists' understanding of the foundations of their own political systems. This striking result, in respect to democracy and stability and the assumptions about the representative nature of government, put into a new perspective the tasks of nation building and suggested a deeper affinity than might have been expected between the First and Third worlds. This same lesson is illustrated in Chapter 4 by a brief concluding look at a "deconstructionist" approach to the state (Mitchell, 1991) that argues the state is an illusory phenomenon and that no strict line exists between state and society.

BRINGING THE PEASANT IN

The final present period in this discussion of the stages through which comparative politics has recently passed begins in Chapter 5 with, perhaps unexpectedly, the peasant—or, to look at the matter more generally, with the discovery of politics at the grassroots where real political struggles and accommodations occur. One of the first studies to show this emphasis was James Scott's *The Moral Economy of the Peasant* (1976), which might reasonably be described as the comparativist's version of "the American Voter," in that it directed a spotlight of inquiry upon an area of political life that had not previously been given close empirical attention. Scott postulated peasant life as violently confronted by physical challenges of drought or famine, and defined peasants' response as a moral community that provided a sort of safety net. The innovative phenomenological approach used by Scott to study peasant communities was sufficiently effective to create a lively dispute over just what in fact was taking place in the previously ignored villages.

Another viewpoint on the peasant, discussed in Chapter 5, was Samuel Popkin's *The Rational Peasant* (1979), a work presenting a far bleaker picture than Scott's of the village as the locus of fierce self-interest, suspicion of others, conspiracies against the rich or poor, and outright social war. In such circumstances, Popkin argued, everyone was behaving as rational choice theory predicted, and the marketplace, where it existed, was the only source of at least partial hopes for the persons trapped by rural poverty. Chapter 5 argues that the debate between morality and rationality was overstated, because the two different behavior patterns were created by the same human motives, intersecting with different conditions of land availability and fertility, or the predictability of rainfall, to produce different results. But the confrontation is educational because it constitutes an almost laboratory example of how different theories create different realities as they are applied to real events, and what two competing paradigms look like in practice.

A major work in the state-society perspective discussed in Chapter 5 also began with peasants. Joel Migdal's *Strong Societies and Weak States* (1988), built upon a variety of trends in comparative politics over past decades and suggested a full-scale microanalytic method for comparative research, the "melange" model of human behavior, defining an ongoing multi-sided political struggle for survival within economic, social, and state institutions. The book began, according to Migdal, with a paradox relative to the state, that its presence is observable everywhere even in the most traditional societies, yet its impact is uncertain; this was explained, according to the study, by defining an inverse relationship between the strength of the society and the state. Strong societies, according to Migdal, prevent strong states from forming because no one is willing to give away sufficient power to allow the state to develop; and state personnel are not independently able to seize such power.

The result is not a standoff but an ongoing battle in which all participants struggle to survive in the face of constant challenge. Chapter 5's analysis argues that Migdal's model is particularly interesting because it does not privilege the powers of the state over social groups but puts each on a roughly equal footing, although armed with different resources—some with wealth, some with status, some with official perquisites, some with nothing but numerical strength. While Migdal describes his work only as an essay, not a theory, the melange approach provides a useful balance of conceptual attention, giving space to all kinds of political actors and integrating them within a common framework.

Chapter 5 draws a comparable example of microanalytic technique from the Africa specialist J. Gus Liebenow's *African Politics* (1986), where the author explains the preponderance of military regimes in Africa through a complex interactive process between the colonial powers and the various indigenous elite groups who systematically misinterpreted their pre-independence experience and on that basis seriously miscalculated their future. Colonial experience, Liebenow argued, created an unrealistic set of expectations, and cast future leaders into political roles that ill-prepared them to govern. These problems meant that African elites used military resources in a way that led to conflict with military leaders, and led to cycles of government overthrow and restoration. This radically "political" view of development processes reaffirms the style of such earlier works as Huntington's.

The final set of scholars discussed in Chapter 5 includes the neo-institutionalist or new institutionalist schools, whose work in the microanalysis of individual behavior within institutional environments was first formalized in James March's and Johan Olsen's "The New Institutionalism" (1984), bringing the dialogue in political science full circle by launching a strong attack against the assumptions and approaches first popularized by behavioralists. Yet the March and Olsen thesis was deeply rooted in the behavioral tradition it criticized (Lave and March 1975): The new institutionalism is "new" only because the behavioral period intervened. Following this textbook example of the dialogic quality of scientific progress, Chapter 5 discusses the two major variations of the new institutionalism that are employed in comparative politics research, the historical school and the rational choice school.

Historical, or sociological, new institutionalism is represented by a recent compilation edited by Steinmo, Thelen, and Longstreth (1992), in which contributors discussed the various ways in which political processes in many nations are influenced in major ways by the formal and informal institutions within which the political debate is contained. Such analyses focus usually on national political phenomena and are "story-telling" approaches rather than attempting to advance and test specific theoretical hypotheses. The economic or rational choice version of the new institutionalism takes a narrower track than does the historical form, but many achieve results of wide applicability even while focusing on smaller groups, as shown in Elinor Ostrom's *Governing the Commons* (1990), a study of the self-organizing behavior of a wide variety of European, Asian, and North American societies. Study of small-scale communities enabled Ostrom to analyze the strategies of actors who must combine competition and cooperation in order to further their own and everyone else's interest in the sustainable utilization of common pool resources.

Since comparative politics is, as remarked earlier, an ongoing enterprise within which new developments are constantly taking place, the final Chapter 6 cannot come to permanent conclusions about the nature of contemporary comparative politics, but tries instead to provide guidance into the recognition and construction of workable theories in comparative research. In line with this purpose, the chapter evaluates the theory of oligarchy, a new form of functionalism, and a widened approach to rational choice theories.

POSTSCRIPT

Before starting the pursuit of comparative politics and the search for theoretic understanding of other societies and our own, a word of caution is relevant. This caution involves the term "democracy," which is sometimes used by the unwary as the conceptual core of political science and of comparative politics especially. Two dangers are inherent in this course of action, and both stem from the fact that when you look closely at the matter you find that no one is very clear about exactly what democracy is. All the definitions of democracy are either verbal or egocentric.

Verbal definitions involve rephrasing a term in different ways, such as that democracy involves "free and fair elections," but never facing the necessity for a thorough definition of "free and fair." Egocentric definitions solve problems of this sort with a self-centered syllogism: "We in the U.S. are a democracy, therefore, if country x is like us then it is a democracy." If we took a hard look at our own society, as indeed political scientists specializing in the United States have done, this solution would seem less compelling. Rational choice theorists such as Downs have suggested that American democracy is built upon a combination of self-aggrandizing politicians and ignorant citizens; politics proceeds by office holders "buying" votes through giveaway programs that bankrupt the state. (If you doubt this, try to explain the current budget deficits in all advanced industrial nations in some other way.) Much about the United States is, of course, admirable, and many people in all parts of the world seek to participate in its freedoms; but it is not yet certain that the American model can or should be imposed uncritically on others.

Definitions that seek to select specific aspects of the American political system as criteria for good government often fail because, taken out of context, these specific institutions do not work properly. Multi-party elections in an underdeveloped country are likely to mean only, as one African academic has said, that "we get to choose which people will oppress us." If we wish to pass judgments on the relative success or failure of other governments, a more modest approach would be to ask if they are well-governed.

"Well-governed" is itself as slippery a term as democracy, but at least it is sufficiently novel that we are aware of its ambiguities with a sharpness we do not notice in dealing with the too-familiar "democracy." Well-governed might mean, for a start, that the physical needs of the people (all of them) are reasonably well met in terms of food, housing, and health, and that their economic needs are also met in terms of remunerative productive employment. If this could be achieved under a benevolent despot, would anyone complain? Would anyone want democracy if everything was going well under some other method of government? If democracy involved severe general poverty, would anyone want it at all? The problem with benevolent despotism is not that it does not work well but that it is fragile: Despots turn from benevolence to malevolence, or their children or successors are fools. Elections are a start (compare Nicaragua, Nigeria, Algeria) but not the whole answer.

All these considerations ask the student of comparative politics, of whatever level of experience, to maintain an open mind. We do not yet know what the best form of government is; comparative politics is a discipline that pursues the inquiry in its broadest and deepest form.

REFERENCES

Almond, Gabriel A., and James S. Coleman (Eds.). *The Politics of the Developing Areas.* Princeton: Princeton University Press, 1960.

Almond, Gabriel A., and Sidney Verba. *The Civic Culture.* Princeton: Princeton University Press, 1963.

Berger, Peter, and Thomas Luckmann. *The Social Construction of Reality.* New York: Anchor, 1967.

Campbell, Angus, Philip E. Converse, Warren E. Miller, and Donald E. Stokes. *The American Voter.* New York: John Wiley and Sons, 1964 (1960).

Cardoso, Fernando Henrique, and Enzo Faletto. *Dependency and Development in Latin America.* Berkeley: University of California Press, 1979.

Dahl, Robert A. *Who Governs? Democracy and Power in an American City.* New Haven: Yale University Press, 1961.

Downs, Anthony. *An Economic Theory of Democracy.* New York: Harper and Row, 1957.

Evans, Peter B., Dietrich Rueschemeyer, and Theda Skocpol (Eds.) *Bringing the State Back in.* New York: Cambridge University Press, 1985.

Evans, Peter B. "Foreign Capital and the Third World State." In Myron Weiner and Samuel Huntington, *Understanding Political Development.* Glenville: Scott Foresman, 1987.

Huntington, Samuel P. *Political Order in Changing Societies.* New Haven: Yale University Press, 1968.

Kuhn, Thomas S. *The Structure of Scientific Revolutions.* Chicago: University of Chicago Press, 1962.

Lane, Jan-Erik, and Svante O. Ersson. *Politics and Society in Western Europe.* Newbury Park: Sage, 1991 (First edition 1987).

Lave, Charles A., and James G. March. *An Introduction to Models in the Social Sciences.* New York: Harper and Row, 1975.

Lerner, Daniel. *The Passing of Traditional Society: Modernizing the Middle East.* New York: Free Press, 1958.

Liebenow, J. Gus. *African Politics: Crises and Challenges.* Bloomington: Indiana University Press, 1986.

Lipset, Seymour Martin. *Political Man: The Social Basis of Politics.* New York: Doubleday Anchor, 1959.

Macridis, Roy C. *The Study of Comparative Government.* New York: Random House, 1955.

March, James G., and Johan P. Olsen. "The New Institutionalism: Organizational Factors in Political Life." *The American Political Science Review* 78 (1984): 734–49.

Migdal, Joel S. *Strong Societies and Weak States: State-Society Relations and State Capabilities in The Third World.* Princeton: Princeton University Press, 1988.

Mitchell, Timothy. "The Limits of the State: Beyond Statist Approaches and Their Critics." *American Political Science Review* 85, no. 1 (March 1991): 77–96.

Moore, Barrington, Jr. *The Social Origins of Dictatorship and Democracy.* Boston: Beacon Press, 1966.

O'Donnell, Guillermo. *Bureaucratic Authoritarianism: Argentina 1966–1973 in Comparative Perspective*. Berkeley: University of California Press, 1988.

Ostrom, Elinor. *Governing the Commons: The Evolution of Institutions for Collective Action*. Cambridge: Cambridge University Press, 1990.

Popkin, Samuel L. *The Rational Peasant: The Political Economy of Rural Society in Vietnam*. Berkeley: University of California Press, 1979.

Scott, James C. *The Moral Economy of the Peasant*. New Haven: Yale University Press, 1976.

Skocpol, Theda. *States and Social Revolutions*. Cambridge: Cambridge University Press, 1979.

Steinmo, Sven, Kathleen Thelen, and Frank Longstreth. *Structuring Politics: Historical Institutionalism in Comparative Analysis*. Cambridge: Cambridge University Press, 1992.

Wallerstein, Immanuel. *The Modern World System: Capitalist Agriculture and the Origins of The European World Economy in the 16th Century*. New York: Academic Press, 1974.

► 2

The Behavioral
Revolution and
Comparative Politics

The behavioral revolution was the defining event in contemporary political science in general, and in the field of comparative politics in particular. As an earthquake, hurricane, or a war affects everything within a given territory, creating hazards and subjecting everyone, high and low, to new experiences, so an intellectual revolution pushes everyone around. The basic premise of the behavioral revolution in political science sounds on its surface simple enough: It was that political science could be, should be, and very shortly would be a scientific discipline. The catch in the argument was that science was hard to define—even physicists have trouble grasping the essence of their trade at any philosophical level, and for social scientists, the newest arrivals at the enterprise, the difficulties were extreme.[1]

At the least, science seemed to political scientists to involve empirical investigations and theoretical explanations: Hard facts should be found (empiricism) and should be summarized in formal propositions (theory building) . The more enthusiastic among the political science community felt that if these principles were adopted, then knowledge about politics would grow in an orderly, cumulative way, until somewhere down the road political science would be fully scientific in nature. Along the frontiers of behavioral political science there was widespread adoption of a scientific metaphysic called positivism, which emphasized the collection of empirical data and the rigorous testing of theoretical propositions against this data. For a brief period of time it seemed that all the troops had lined up under the same inspiring banner, and that they were marching in unity toward the future.[2]

Revolutions are complex events, however: Many ideas that look good on the first day of the revolution do not work quite as expected when the second day rolls around and the new order must be put into actual practice. The "enemy" the revolutionary be-havioralists faced was not so much the unconverted "old-fashioned" scientists, who for a time were swept along in the euphoria or who maintained a discreet silence on the great methodological issues. The enemy was politics itself—how to grasp this roaring, raging, combative, devious, idealistic, world-making, world-destroying phe-nomenon in some scientific conceptualization. It was one thing to be in favor of sci-entific approaches, and rather another thing to invent ways of carrying this program into actual practice.[3]

Because no one today can understand comparative politics without first under-standing the behavioral revolution in political science, the present chapter inquires into some of the major books that defined the movement not only in comparative studies but in the wider discipline of political science itself. The diversity of these "behavioral" works is, in retrospect, awesome. The question of what these works could have had in common, to justify their being lumped into a single movement, re-mains an interesting issue.

First on the list of the works that served to define behavioralism in practice was *The American Voter* (Campbell, Converse, Miller, and Stokes, 1964), which redefined political science permanently. Related in comparative politics to this innovation in survey research was *The Civic Culture* (Almond and Verba, 1963), a study of demo-cratic and social attitudes in five nations. Both works based themselves on the col-lection of masses of empirical data derived from mass public opinion polling, and both found it difficult to develop new theory to replace the "outdated" traditional ideas about how citizens should behave.

Demonstrating how strange were the bedfellows of the behavioral revolution, the discussion then turns from atheoretical empiricism to abstract economic reasoning in Downs' *An Economic Theory of Democracy* (1957), which added to the undermining of the older attitudes about democratic virtues by showing that an explanatory model premised on the most cynical self-interest on the part of both public officials and vot-ers was highly effective in predicting behavior.

A further component of the behavioral revolution is illustrated by Seymour Mar-tin Lipset's sociological study, *Political Man* (1963), characterized by aggregate data and a class-based analysis that sought the foundations of democratic stability in the socioeconomic conditions of developed societies. Another sociological approach that took a quite different place in the behavioral canon was Robert Dahl's *Who Governs?* (1961), a sociological case study of a local political system.

In some contrast to these diverse participants in the behavioral revolution, the chapter concludes with Easton's systems theory, which took a major role at the theo-retical level, and with a summary of Easton's "behavioral creed," which gave the movement more unity than it may in fact have possessed. The overall thesis of the chapter is that the stereotype of behavioralism should not deter comparativists from learning its lessons, which were much more varied than is sometimes recognized.

To begin to understand the dynamics of political science during the behavioral period, and in the present, it is necessary to bear in mind not only general movements but individual diversity, not only what the participants agreed about, but their differences—the struggle implicit in their scholarly debates. The controversies of the political science discipline are relevant to the student of comparative politics because at every battle, in every trench, at every strategic hill, comparativists played a major role.

THE REACTION TO THE PAST

What was this "traditional" political science that made it such a bugbear to the behavioralists? The indictment against traditional political science was summed up in 1955 by Roy Macridis, a comparativist influenced by the tradition's patent failure to deal with new conditions in the post-colonial international world. Traditional political science, Macridis argued, had shown its inadequacy in the practical political world; it gave no direction for policy making and it was not applicable to nonwestern societies. Worse, it was not comparative, which made it impossible to develop generalized theories about political behavior (1955, pp. 7–22).

These failures resulted, according to Macridis and other critics of the old ways, from several aspects of the discipline as traditionally practiced.[4] First, traditional political science was accused of being descriptive ("merely descriptive" was the scornful phrase of the time). But, on second thought, all agreed that traditional political science was not even properly descriptive, because it studied only very narrow aspects of government, and indeed often focused on matters that were not even facts, such as how the constitution said a government should run, quite ignoring that the government did not actually operate in the prescribed manner. Finally, critics began to sense that, much of the time, traditional political science did not attend to the real world at all, but to ideas, to the political scientists' beliefs about how political scientists thought governments should be run. This led to an unfortunate tendency for such traditionalists to twist the facts in order to show that their favorite government system actually did meet these idealistic standards. This was a major cause of the behavioralists' rejection of comparative politics as it was traditionally practiced.

THE ACTUAL REVOLUTION

Intellectual revolutions, like political ones, are not disembodied abstract events but are grounded in particular people. What appears in retrospect as "a" revolution was at the time it occurred not unified in intent but the result of the concurrent work of many separate individuals, individuals who agreed in rejecting the past but who did not necessarily agree in their specific vision for the future. The behavioral revolution proceeded under some well-known names, and even more under the influence of some well-known books—books that the political science community acknowledged as representing the new frontier that they were committed to explore.

One of the first of these was *The American Voter* (Campbell et al., 1960, 1964), which had so overwhelming an influence on the behavioral movement that its importance cannot be overstated. The approach the book embodied seemed to be the very perfection of all the scientific canons the discipline wished to pursue. Vast data collection using the most current survey methods allowed researchers to analyze representative samples of the population and to employ increasingly sophisticated statistical tools to generate and test hypotheses about political behavior, not only voting behavior but participatory activities and political attitudes. In addition, there were rich series of questions on education, income, religious beliefs, occupation, and so on. The Michigan surveys formed the core of a vast and expanding body of data collected now under the auspices of the Inter-University Consortium for Political and Social Research, and made available, along with statistical training, to subsequent generations of political scientists.[5]

The use of opinion surveys had begun earlier, with such works as *The People's Choice* (Lazarsfeld, Berelson, and Gaudet, 1948), a sociological study of voting in Erie County, Ohio, but the approach taken by scholars at the University of Michigan's Survey Research Center became the standard for political science research. In what came to be called the "political psychology" approach, Campbell and his colleagues used not only socioeconomic data but a battery of psychological attitude questions, including voter orientations to political parties and candidates, the voters' sense of citizenship, their interest in politics, opinions on foreign and domestic policy issues, and most important of all, the voters' partisan identification, the political party to which each adhered. The authors found, overall, a "low emotional involvement of the electorate in politics; its slight awareness of public affairs; its failure to think in structured, ideological terms; and its pervasive sense of attachment to one or the other of the two major parties" (Campbell et al., 1964, pp. 280–281).

From these characteristics, the authors developed three consequences for the larger political system of which such voters were a part: first, that voters did not express policy in their voting behavior, and that leaders had great latitude in forming policy as a result; second, that candidates relied far more on personality than on ideology during campaigns; and third, that the electorate's attitudes cemented into place the two-party system because voter loyalty barred third parties from success, and discontent with the party in office maintained a vigorous opposition (Campbell et al., 1964, pp. 282–288).[6]

The impact of the National Election Studies was to change political science forever. Not only did the survey approach represent a "microscope" for looking at grassroots behavior that had never before been given serious attention, but what it found at the grassroots revised everyone's ideas of democratic government. If democracy required citizens that were well-informed, consistent in their beliefs, and capable of some concern for the public welfare, then survey research suggested the idea of democracy might be in trouble, since the citizens, to put it kindly, were ill-informed, uninterested in becoming better informed, fuzzy and inconsistent in their beliefs, and devoted to narrow personal concerns. If the task of a new research paradigm is to open a thousand new questions and puzzles, then the Michigan approach amply fulfilled this expectation. Whatever criticisms would be made of survey research over the years, both from outside and inside the school, its early successes cannot be denied.[7]

SURVEY RESEARCH ON AN INTERNATIONAL SCALE

If *The American Voter* was the shot heard round the political science world announcing the onset of the behavioral revolution, a book in comparative politics appeared about the same time that seemed to outdistance it by a factor of five (Almond and Verba, 1963) . Not only did *The Civic Culture* use the latest techniques of sampling and survey research, but it extended this methodology beyond the United States to include Britain, Germany, Italy, and Mexico. The sheer organizational triumph of such a cross-national survey was impressive: A conceptual focus needed to be found that would be relevant to a wide variety of nations, including one from the underdeveloped world; questions had to be formulated, tested, and translated into other languages and cultures without losing their meaning and nuance; interviewers had to be hired and trained; and the whole widespread enterprise administered. This was worthy of admiration. Political scientists marveled, and graduate students recounted probably apocryphal stories of the hazards encountered in the field, such as irate Italian husbands chasing interviewers from their doors.

The Civic Culture was born famous and remained famous. Closer consideration of the work, therefore, contains several lessons about the behavioral revolution, about political science in general, and about comparative politics in particular. In looking at examples of research from the behavioral period, one important aspect is their role as "models" of research, showing how the leaders of the discipline behaved when doing actual research rather than merely writing in the abstract about how it "should" be done. Here *The Civic Culture* was both awesome in its accomplishment and stultifying in its effect. If, in order to do "good" research in comparative politics, the researcher was required to do full-scale surveys in five different nations, then there were very few who could even aspire to such glory. So *The Civic Culture* was a shining and unattainable goal for most comparativists.[8]

On the other hand, the conceptual approach taken in the study left many readers discontented, and the empirical findings raised a variety of questions. Even the books's authors did not express great satisfaction with *The Civic Culture,* and this ambivalence suggested that the technical triumph of the work was greater than its substantive result. Intellectual inquiry, Almond and Verba said in an introductory chapter, should allow the mind to "come to rest" on some conclusions; but they confessed that, for its authors, their study of the civic culture had not had this effect.[9]

The idea of culture was defined by Almond and Verba as a narrowed version of that used by anthropologists, and involved a "psychological orientation toward social objects." Political culture was defined as "the political system as internalized in the cognitions, feelings, and evaluations of its population" (Almond and Verba, 1963, pp. 8, 14) . The most recent antecedents of the cultural idea in political science had been the ideas of "modal personality" or "national character" used by some social scientists, often in works for a popular audience, to explain how all or most of the people in a certain country behaved in their own peculiar ways, unlike the ways of persons in other countries.[10] Anyone who has ever explained the apparently odd behavior of someone by saying "Well, you know, all the French are like that" has fallen into this mode of explanation.

GOING BEYOND THE CIVICS TEXTBOOKS

The Civic Culture took a higher perspective, presenting a developmentally based model in which there were three types of citizens: participants, who took active part in the political process by voting and group activities; subjects, who were oriented to the output sides of government, such as obeying the laws and paying taxes, but not active policy participation; and parochials, who largely ignored government. The initial expectation that Americans and the English would be fully participant, with other countries falling further and further down the development scale with respect to the type of citizenship, turned out to be unrealistic. The authors of *The Civic Culture* therefore modified their theory, in an unobtrusive but excellent example of the way in which survey research did serve rigorously to test hypotheses and reject those that failed.

The "civic culture" was finally defined not as pure participation but as a mixing of the other types (Almond and Verba, 1963, p. 20). Along with the rationality-activist model described in civics textbooks, the civic culture added the idea of allegiance, a positive orientation "to the input structures and the input process" and a retention of subject and parochial political orientations such as trust in people and general social activity, which served to " 'manage' " or keep in place" participatory activity (Almond and Verba, 1963, pp. 31–32) . Perhaps the quickest introduction to the content of the study can be achieved by reviewing some of the interview schedule, which was included in the book's appendix, another practice typical of books written in the period (Almond and Verba, 1963, pp. 526–549).

- All of us have ideas about what people should be like. Here is a list of characteristics you might find in people. Could you select the quality you admire most (and next best)?

    Does job well
    Active in public and social affairs
    Ambitious, wants to get ahead
    Generous, considerate of others
    Thrifty, saving
    Lets no one take advantage of him

> Keeps himself to himself
> Respectful, doesn't overstep his place

- Some people say that most people can be trusted. Others say you can't be too careful. How do you feel about it?
- Of the people you hear or read about, could you name some you admire?
- Here are some important problems facing the people in this country. Would you please read it and tell me which is most important to you personally?

> Spiritual and moral betterment
> Making ends meet
> Government control and regulation of business
> Eliminating inequality and injustice
> Foreign affairs, national defense
> Improving conditions for your family

- Suppose you were trying to influence a governmental decision. Which of the following methods would you be most likely to use?

> Work through family and personal connections
> Write government officials
> Form a group of interested people
> Work through a political party
> Organize a protest demonstration

- Have you ever actually tried to change a law? If you have not, do you believe you would succeed?
- How do you feel about voting?

> Feeling of satisfaction
> Just do my duty
> Waste of time, annoyance
> Nothing

- Did you have much influence when you were growing up in family decisions? If you complained, was there a response?
- Did you discuss things a lot in school? Were you treated fairly?
- Do you agree or disagree: "The way people vote is the main thing that decides how things are run in this country."
- Do you agree or disagree: "If you don't watch yourself people will take advantage of you."
- Do you agree or disagree: "Candidates sound good in their speeches but you can never tell what they will do after they are elected."

The data derived from questions as rich as these, in the wide context of five different nations, obviously provided a mother-lode of intriguing information; the problem was to organize it and integrate it into some explanatory framework. Almond and Verba began by looking at the cognitive factors involved in cultural behavior.[11] Instead of full cognitive maps the authors took a limited subset of factors: the citizen's level of political information, awareness of politics and public affairs, the ability to formulate political opinions, and the attribution of importance to public affairs.

As in the *American Voter* studies, the results of the five-nation study were not encouraging for those who might believe that the United States was a highly participant democracy: Of the Americans, for instance, only 43 percent followed campaigns, and only 27 percent followed government affairs regularly. In the matter of following public affairs, indeed, the Germans scored higher (34 percent) than the Americans, leading the authors rather grudgingly to admit that Germany perhaps had "civic tendencies," contrary to hypothesis (Almond and Verba, 1963, pp. 79–89) . When it came to citizens' ability to identify national leaders of various sorts, the data showed the English and the Italians both low on the scale, a result that again violated the expectations of anyone who held the stereotyped view of England as the most democratically advanced nation, with Italy lagging well behind. Another set of expectations was overturned by the Mexicans, who were expected as citizens of a Third World nation to be parochial, but who proved to be surprisingly articulate in their political opinions (Almond and Verba, 1963, p. 96). Moving beyond cognition to feelings, *The Civic Culture* inquired into generalized attitudes to the "system as a whole" and to expectations about treatment of citizens by government officials; in the jargon of the study these were "system affect" and "output affect" respectively.

Beyond system affect, the study inquired into feelings toward individual parties, but the questions, diluted to make them span several countries, were crude (Would you be willing to have your child marry a member of the x party?) and the results not interesting (Almond and Verba, 1963, pp. 125–130). On the obligation to participate, the authors concluded that it was impossible anyway to determine what the ideal level of participation was for a democracy; perhaps low participation was beneficial for stability (Chapter 6) . They resorted to a "capillary" image for the body politic, in which the "flush of good health" was produced by the meshing of diffuse citizen feelings with differentiated political structures to create the sense of legitimacy. The "great act of mass participation" was, from this viewpoint, the act of voting rather than any of the more obstreperous forms that participation might take, such as demonstrations or unconventional political activity (see a recent review of the issues in Nelson, 1987).

THE RESPONSE TO THE CIVIC CULTURE STUDY

Any book so full of political detail was open on every page to criticism, and *The Civic Culture* was not ignored. It became such an institution within the discipline that in 1980 a "sequel" was published, called *The Civic Culture Revisited,* which combined some of these criticisms with retrospective remarks by the original authors. The failure adequately to define the meaning of political culture was a major cause of complaint: The various questionnaire items were interesting in themselves but did not cohere in terms of any internal logic. Almond defended the work against this problem by referring to another volume published the same year (Pye and Verba, 1963) but that book took a different approach in many ways and did not provide an appropriate answer.

Two related criticisms involved the analytic distinction between political culture and political structure, and *The Civic Culture's* assumption that the causal arrow went from culture to structure. Here the critics had a strong case. *The Civic Culture* often proceeds as if "civic" citizens created good government. The Italians, for instance, were characterized not as good "allegiant" citizens but as "alienated," and there is an interesting tendency by the authors to overlook the possibility that alienation might be a perfectly rational attitude within some political systems, rather than a fault of the citizens who, had they been more allegiant, would have somehow created a better government for themselves.[12]

But the present interest in *The Civic Culture* is not diminished by specific complaints, to which any ambitious research program may be open. Rather the concern is for what the work tells students of comparative politics about the practical shape of the behavioral revolution as it worked itself out in important books of the period. The first lesson here must be the difficulty of finding not just theories but even conceptual frameworks adequate to explain one's data. It is admirable and progressive to collect data as a way of testing theories and ideas; it is often more difficult to find theories worth testing. *The Civic Culture* may have failed to satisfy those who sought a theory about political culture adequate to answer present questions and to guide future research. It is, however, not always sufficiently appreciated how many older ideas were demolished by *The Civic Culture* and similar works. A brief look backwards shows how extensive was this change.

The intellectual origins of Almond's work lay in his training at the University of Chicago, and the research climate defined there by Charles Merriam.[13] For political scientists, a major dimension of this climate was Merriam's concern with civic virtue and the need to train citizens in such virtue, which was the foundation of stable democratic government. What this involves is not scientific research but old-fashioned "civics" education: teaching people to love their country, to admire its institutions, to obey its laws, to love its symbols, to honor its history, to fulfill the roles allotted to them, and to protect all these goods against any challenger. *The Civic Culture* was in effect two books, linked together by force as well as reason. The first book was about how a good citizen should behave, according to classic writers like Aristotle, and to the authors of *The Civic Culture* itself, whose ideas on American democracy stemmed from prebehavioral roots. The second book was a report on research carried out in the most modern of survey styles, yet conceptualized on traditional lines. The second book largely demolished the first. People do not behave in the manner to which they have been exhorted. This was the often-ignored lesson of *The Civic Culture*. It left political scientists facing a host of questions, many of which they were afraid to ask, about how democracy really works when the citizens are not virtuous in the old sense.

THE ECONOMIC THEORY OF DEMOCRACY

A work quite unlike the survey research approach but one that was equally of prime importance in the behavioral movement was Anthony Downs' *An Economic Theory of Democracy* (1957). Downs' book on democracy was not initially greeted as a major element of the behavioral revolution; the main national political science journal never even reviewed it. Nevertheless *An Economic Theory of Democracy* made its own way by the sheer acuity of its analysis, and achieved a remarkable ascendancy, creating a cottage industry over the question of whether it was or was not rational for a citizen to vote, and participating with other early works in political economy in the construction of perhaps the strongest theoretic approach ever to flourish within the fields of political science.[14] Downs's argument may today have become so familiar that its revolutionary nature is hard for current readers to appreciate. But if his conclusions now appeal naturally to younger generations, there is still a lesson inherent in the work about the internal logic that made traditionalists, forty years ago, unable to resist his attack, which came clothed in just enough economic theory to make it invincible without making it difficult.

Downs' argument in *An Economic Theory of Democracy* has a coherence rare in political science. His goals were set out as the discovery of a general equilibrium theory, the explanation or at least the prediction of political behavior, and a search for the rational basis of political order. The method employed was the economic approach, based on the assumption of rational behavior by individuals. Rationality was defined according to three criteria: that behavior was directed by goals, that it was based on self-interest, and that in his particular analysis rationality would be related only to government selection (Downs, 1957, pp. 4–7).

The basic model included small groups, such as parties and interest groups, and individual voters. They acted within a highly simplified but not necessarily oversimplified political system based on eight rules that defined a basic democratic structure: All adults were allowed to vote, each got one vote, there were two or more political parties, elections were held periodically, a single party or coalition was chosen by election, in counting votes the party that received the majority was declared the winner, the losers did not try to prevent the winners from taking office, and the winners did not attempt to wipe out the losers (unless they were guilty of treason) (Downs, 1957, pp. 23–24).

Having stripped down the institutional structure to its bare minimum, and having laid his axioms, Downs began to work out their implications for the political process. His fundamental hypothesis, following from the general assumption about rationality, was that political parties formed policies only to win votes, and that voters voted for whomever would give them the greatest benefits. This, of course, cast illusions about "the public interest" out the window, and sent hopes for a virtuous citizenry after them. Government decision making, according to Downs, was based on marginal expenditure: Programs would be increased until the vote gain from each dollar spent equaled the loss of votes resulting from increased taxes. The governing party's best strategy was simply to find out what the majority of voters wanted and to do it; the opposition's best strategy was exactly the same except that they had to promise to do it better than the government (Downs, 1957, pp. 52–55).

THE PROBLEM OF COLLECTIVE CHOICE

Individual decision making was based in Downs' system on the calculus of the party differential. The voter compared the benefits that would accrue to him or her from each of the parties, and voted for whichever party paid off with the highest utility. The voter also took into consideration the parties' performance on their promises, whether, the promises being the same, one party was more efficient, or one party seemed to be improving. All this was made rather more complicated by the problems of information gathering, as Downs showed later in the argument.

The Arrow Paradox was then introduced to show the difficulty of producing rational social choices. If there are three voters with the preferences shown below, where the first option is preferred to the second, and so on, then it was clear that (1) that a simple majority vote would produce no result at all (each option would receive one vote), and that (2) voting by pairs would yield "cyclical" majorities, where the outcome would depend on the order in which the votes were taken.

Voter 1	Voter 2	Voter 3
A	B	C
B	C	A
C	A	B

If the group first voted between A or B, that is, A would win; if it voted between B or C, then B would win; and if the group voted between C or A, then C would win. This meant simply that there was a political situation for which there was no rational solution (Downs, 1957, pp. 60–62).

The solution Downs suggested was uncertainty or ignorance, without which, he said, democracy might be impossible. Uncertainty involved three levels: information or current facts, knowledge of context, and reason or understanding; and it divided people into classes because it was unevenly distributed. The fact that people are divided into information-based classes gives rise, according to Downs, to the possibility of persuasion, as parties give out selected information in order to attract voters; and to the need for political intermediaries, to find out what the voters want (Downs, 1957, p. 87) . Because the information gathering process is so complex, involving locating facts, analyzing them, sifting them for validity, and so on, the next stage of the argument postulated that voters would find it rational to delegate these tasks to specialists.

In a final creative leap, Downs defined leadership as the specialty of influencing those people who needed to be relieved of uncertainty. To achieve this, leaders report the news, set political fashions, and shape cultural images of good and evil. The leaders' ideologies are not to be taken at face value but are considered to be weapons in the struggle for office, according to Downs. The ideologies give voters alternative verbal images of the good society and the leaders' proposed methods of bringing about this society. Ideologies also constrain the leaders because voters come to value consistency, and ideology is a way of predicting how a leader will decide issues in the future (Downs, 1957, pp. 96–113).

THE DISAPPEARANCE OF RATIONALITY

This set the stage for the final phase of Downs' theoretical drama. Assuming that voters' preferences are arranged in the usual bell-shaped curve, with most people clustering in the moderate center of the scale, tapering off to fewer people at the right and left ends, Downs adopted a spatial model to show that it is rational for political leaders to direct their appeals to the center area, and that the best way to do this is to clothe one's appeals in the fuzziest possible language, so that the widest possible range of voters will be attracted. But when politicians use this sort of appeal, the voters cannot tell what their actual utilities will be, and so cannot vote according to their self-interest. This led to the unhappy conclusion that when politicians are acting rationally, they make it impossible for the voters to act rationally. The system is therefore inconsistent and the search for the rational basis of the political order, postulated as a goal of the study, has failed (Downs, 1957, p. 257).

There is a great deal more to the argument, which Downs takes into multiparty systems, where the situation is even more difficult for rational voters, but this skeleton is sufficient to introduce the economic approach to anyone who has somehow escaped it hitherto. The particular characteristic of such analyses is that once the assumptions are accepted, everything else is a slippery slope to the conclusion. And if the early reader was immune to the power of logic, he was faced in addition with the result of comparing Downs's predictions with everyday political reality, and finding inescapable resemblances. The whole modern welfare state could be interpreted as bribery by various politicians who gave social programs in return for votes; and politicians notoriously geared their speeches to say as little as possible that could offend, or enlighten, the voters. Nor was there much evidence that the old ideas of civic virtue among voters—the idea of self-discipline and a recognition of the rights of other persons than oneself—could withstand Downs's and others' pictures of political man as rationally greedy.

An Economic Theory of Democracy was enormously influential, clearing away large amounts of traditional underbrush, but it was also a kind of dead end. Rather than taking up some of Downs' most ingenious innovations, and going on to ask the question of exactly how one might analyze, for instance, the idea of leaders as arbiters of good and evil, many political scientists settled down to endless discussions over whether voters were rational, using elegant mathematical techniques where common sense might have served better. The possibility that theory of the Downsian sort might be a solution to the search for general theory gradually diminished, as economic theorizing became a narrow field of study for those who approved of its assumptions, while those who disagreed with the economic approach attacked it from all directions without ever diminishing the enthusiasm of its advocates. For many years, however, rational choice theory in its various forms, continued to serve as the epitome of what good theory should be, even among those who did not practice it.[15]

POLITICAL MAN AND POLITICAL SOCIOLOGY

When revolutions occur, there will be at least a few people who do not directly participate at the barricades but come to be participants because the work in which they were individually engaged was reflective of the principles upon which the revolution was based. Seymour Martin Lipset, who published in 1960 the widely read *Political Man,* is a case in point. Working within an older tradition of comparative political sociology, Lipset's heavy reliance on empirical data made his work fully compatible with behavioralism; as did his primary normative concern with discovering those conditions and processes that were conducive to democratic development. What set *Political Man* apart was its semi-Marxist emphasis on social class as relevant to democratic development, and its emphasis on conflict as a pre-eminent characteristic of social and political behavior. Lipset's conclusions were not markedly different from those of the more mainstream writers, but his analysis had a sharper European edge to it, recalling old class wars and historic social animosities.

The first stage of analysis in *Political Man* dealt with the economic foundations of democracy, noting the strong positive correlation between capitalist industrialization and democracy (despite such failures as Germany in the period between the world wars) . The generalization that "wealth fosters democracy" was explored with socioeconomic data such as per capita income, persons per motor vehicle, physicians per thousands of population, and so on; particular note was given to the correlations between democracy and levels of education within a nation (Lipset, 1960, pp. 28–31). Industrialization, urbanization, wealth, and education were all intertwined; and there was a negative correlation of these variables with class struggle. The wealthiest countries had no socialists, according to Lipset, and poor countries alone were radical (Lipset, 1960, p. 45) . He found the "correlates" of democracy to be an open class system, an egalitarian value system, literacy, and a high participation in voluntary organizations, along with capitalism and wealth; but these were consequences as well, and the direction of causation could not be clearly determined (Lipset, 1960, p. 61).

Lipset gave special attention to the fundamental way in which his approach differed from mainstream individualistic approaches. Political man was not an atomistically isolated individual, he said, but was embedded in social systems, social classes, social organizations; in an earlier work, for instance, Lipset had explored democracy in labor unions (Lipset, Trow, and Coleman, 1956) . But he also placed great emphasis on his differences with older political sociologies that separated "ideal types" of social organizations from their complex realities. While Lipset advocated strong theoretical perspectives, he required that the theories be derivable from and testable by the empirical data. This is what made him such an appropriate companion for the behavioral movement (see his "methodological appendix," Lipset, 1960, pp. 58-62).

DEMOCRACY AND STABILITY

An equally important characteristic Lipset shared with other political scientists of the period was his central concern with political stability; this was perhaps to be expected in a century which by its midpoint had experienced a Bolshevik revolution, a catastrophic worldwide depression, and two world wars. Whatever the reasons, many writers on democracy were equally interested in stability. According to Lipset, stability is the result of two factors, effectiveness and legitimacy. Political effectiveness he defined as the satisfaction by the government of those functions required by the population as a whole but perhaps more importantly by powerful groups such as big business and the military (Lipset, 1960, p. 64).

Political legitimacy, which he argued might exist with many forms of government, including oppressive ones, is based on a popular belief that the existing political institutions express the citizens' values and are the most appropriate institutions for the group. Countries can then be classified according to the fourfold table created by the intersection of these two dimensions. Some countries are both effective and legitimate (the United States, Sweden, Britain); others are legitimate but not effective (the European countries that survived as democracies in the 1930s); others are effective but not legitimate ("well-governed colonies"); and some are neither effective nor legitimate (the Eastern European countries of the 1950s) (Lipset, 1960, pp. 68–69). In passing, it may be remarked that since Aristotle's classification of governments, political scientists have sought to "explain" political systems by putting them into various classificatory systems; most of these attempts have failed to accomplish the purpose any better than did those of Aristotle.

Lipset's dynamic theory of democracy in *Political Man* is that stable democracy is the result both of cleavage and consensus in society; he labels this "polyarchy" (Lipset, 1960, p. 1). Cleavage meant economic cleavage creating different groups within economic society, groups that were in conflict with one another and were therefore driven to organize themselves in order to participate effectively in that conflict. In this way conflict (among groups) creates unity (within groups) and through this process of conflict structured through democratic institutions, development of the whole system occurs. This is the American echo of the hypothesis that "history is the history of class conflict." Consensus, on the other hand, is something that emerges from the conflict in a way Marx never intended, an attitude of tolerance on the part of the participants toward one another, so that their conflict is constrained within manageable bounds and stability is enhanced (Lipset, 1960, p. 2).

Ideally the process of voting is a key mechanism in creating consensus, according to Lipset. Even though we often study voting from the cleavage perspective—blue collar workers on one side of an issue, managers and owners, on the other—political issues engender consensus because they cross class lines in many different ways, Lipset argued. When everyone within the political system, rich and poor alike, responds the same way to major stimuli, this indicates high consensus (Lipset, 1960, pp. 12–15). Lipset sees however a much darker set of possibilities. Cleavage between major conservative institutions and politically excluded groups may occur that are not surmounted by the consensus process (p. 65), and there are many threats to democratic stability, from working class authoritarianism (p. 126) to the insecure, intolerant middle and upper classes (pp. 65, 126, 178–179). High voting participation, so often defined as a desirable aspect of democracy, may be a sign of discontent. But if people fail to vote, their consent cannot be counted upon. Thus, democracy emerges from Lipset's analysis as a paradox.

DEMOCRACY AND MASS SOCIETY

What does *Political Man* tell the contemporary political scientists about the behavioral revolution of which it formed a part? One lesson, which should be obvious but is not always so, is that the collection and analysis of empirical data is not a neutral practice. A school of political scientists, sometimes called "barefoot" empiricists, tends to believe that if data are collected with sufficient assiduity they will "speak" to the investigator and provide fundamental truths uninfected by any theoretical commitment. *Political Man* shows the weakness of such an idea. The type of data the investigator chooses does not come without long chains of intellectual commitments and implicit theories dragging behind. What marks *Political Man* is its European assumption that social class matters. American political scientists have not ordinarily been comfortable with this hypothesis; at least in part because the behavioral period was very close in time to the McCarthy Era in American politics, when it was advisable to avoid anything that might sound, to a suspicious ear, subversive.

A second dimension of Lipset's *Political Man* is its connection with a long European tradition that has had profound doubts about democracy and democratic government. Americans are almost wholly insensitive to the suggestion that "mass society" might be a bad thing, representing lack of culture, lack of civilization, lack of intellectual tradition, lack of "breeding." Democracy, from this point of view, is government by the vulgar. Lipset's reflections on the working classes, with their possibly fascist proclivities (Lipset, 1960, p. 126), suggest the strength of this tradition; a tradition quite unlike the typical American's eighteenth century belief in human equality, in progress and prosperity, and in the timeless validity of democracy.[16] Lipset is ultimately ambivalent on the issue, firmly assuming that democracy is a good thing but doubtful about the merits of its citizens. This strain is found in many of the works included in this chapter, including the apparently quite different analysis of local government, which was one of the best known of the behavioral movement's exemplars.

WHO GOVERNS?

Robert Dahl's *Who Governs?* (1961) was a major star in the constellation that made up the behavioral movement. A second look at this political science classic can aid in defining what behavioralism was and was not. On first consideration, a study of politics in a decaying city in southern Connecticut may seem to be an unlikely candidate for greatness, even if the city houses Yale University. *Who Governs?*, however, fell within a tradition of community power studies by sociologists, such as the Lynds' *Middletown* (1929), Hunter's study of Atlanta (1953) and Warner's *Yankee City* (1963); and was welcomed as the first time a political scientist had undertaken such a work in local government.

The thesis established by the community power studies, and in respect to which Dahl directed a major proportion of his discussion, was the thesis of elite rule: In supposedly democratic America, local communities were governed, explicitly or implicitly, by oligarchies.[17] Dahl's study sought to refute the idea of a single dominant elite, but the book's fame may have resulted more importantly from a good political tale, well told. If prebehavioral writers had been chastised for dealing in abstract dissertations on constitutions without attention to actual politics, Dahl's approach to New Haven was richly concrete. From Richard Lee, the mayor who achieved national attention for his urban redevelopment policies, to Miss Mary Grava, who launched a successful campaign to drive slumlords from her neighborhood, the specific names, specific politics, specific ethnic and specific socioeconomic identities are all present, and in profusion, in *Who Governs?*

Dahl's method in the study of New Haven was primarily sociological; he did not focus on policy so much as on the leaders who governed at various periods of the city's history, and on their sociological and economic characteristics. This approach divided the rule of New Haven into three periods: first, the patrician rulers (1793 to 1839) who were from "the established families" and combined high economic, educational, and cultural resources; then, the entrepreneurs (1842 to 1897), "self-made" businessmen who came from humble beginnings but achieved wealth and political power; and finally, what Dahl called the "ex-plebes" (1899 to 1953), who had no status at all except their ability to garner votes (Dahl, 1961, pp. 12–14). Summarizing these changes, Dahl presented his major argument, that the change in New Haven was "from the old pattern of oligarchy based upon *cumulative* inequalities to new patterns of leadership based upon *dispersed* inequalities" (Dahl, 1961, p. 51, emphasis added). Three issue areas were used to investigate influence patterns, (1) party nominations, (2) urban redevelopment, and (3) schools and educational policy. The conclusion was the foundation of pluralist theory, that different elites were dominant in the different issue areas studied.

In reference to the initial question whether an economic elite dominated New Haven, Dahl concluded neither that notables governed nor that they were powerless; rather, like all other active participants, the economic forces in the city were effective in some areas of policy and not in others (Dahl, 1961, p. 72).

> As with other groups, the likelihood of getting their way is a complex function of many factors: the relevance to political influence of the resources at their disposal; the extent to which the group members agree; their application, persistence, and skill; the amount and kinds of opposition they generate; the degree to which their objectives are viewed as consistent with the political aims of elected leaders; and the extent to which their aims are consistent with widespread beliefs in the community (1961, p. 75).

EXECUTIVE EXCITEMENT

Sociology was not the whole story of *Who Governs?*, however. New Haven would perhaps not even have been considered worthy of study, despite its convenient proximity to Yale, had it not contained an "ex-plebe" of extraordinary dimensions, Richard C. Lee, elected mayor at the age of 37, and the major force behind the city's downtown renewal project. There are many reasons why *Who Governs?* had no successors in other American cities, but the scarcity of stylish city executives was certainly among them. Instead of the city bosses, wardheelers, and political nonentities ruling other cities, New Haven boasted a tweed-jacketed, bow-tied, crewcut mayor without a college education but, as the former director of public relations for Yale, with all the necessary academic connections. The mayor and his urban renewal program were clearly the heroes of the tale:

> He possessed a large repertoire of political skills and an unusual ability to perform a variety of different roles. His political skills included a talent for public relations that played no small part in developing his national reputation. He had an investment banker's willingness to take risks that held the promise of large long-run payoffs, and a labor mediator's ability to head off controversy by searching out areas for agreement by mutual understanding, compromise, negotiation, and bargaining. He possessed a detailed knowledge of the city and its people, a formidable information-gathering system, and an unceasing, full-time preoccupation with all the aspects of his job. His

relentless drive to achieve his goals meant that he could be tough and ruth-
less. But toughness was not his political style, for his overriding strategy
was to rely on persuasion rather than threats (p. 119).

The "executive-centered coalition," one of Dahl's five hypothesized patterns of
leadership, was based directly on the experience of New Haven under Mayor Lee. In
the previous city pattern of "petty sovereignties," each issue area was controlled by a
different set of top leaders and the executive was at the center of intersecting circles
of power; in the Lee pattern, a hierarchy prevailed (Dahl, 1961, p. 204). Dahl made
no claim that the new pattern of authority would last; more likely it would be replaced
by petty sovereignties, he said, and be ruled as it had been before. Nonetheless the
figure of Lee is vital to the interest of the study, suggesting as it does the hope that
government may be both successful in its policies and popular with its citizens.

Dahl speculates, on the basis of "various kinds of evidence—all of it, alas, highly
debatable," that the major force for stability is the American creed and the mutual
process by which leaders and citizens mutually negotiate over its norms while not
questioning their foundations. Were this consensus to decline, people might be led
astray by "appeals intended to destroy democracy in the name of democracy" (Dahl,
1961, pp. 315–325).

BEHAVIORAL LESSONS

What does *Who Governs?* tell the retrospective reader about the behavioral movement? Three characteristics stand out as typical of the book and of the movement that
it helped to create. First, *Who Governs?* gave a sense of the opening up of new worlds
for study by giving new legitimacy to a topic—local government—that had never before received attention from political scientists unless they were public administrators. Second, *Who Governs?* defined itself in predominantly sociological terms, being
written within the context defined by Hunter and other sociologists, and continually
emphasizing the social factors that underlay New Haven's political history. Most political scientists, prior to this time, had not chosen to look much beyond government
institutions per se, and a political research project that was so rich in upper and lower
classes, patricians and plebians, Irish and Italian and Russian Jewish politicians and
voters, had the true revolutionary quality.

Associated with the sociological aspects of the study was, third, its empiricism
and emphasis on methods to ensure as much objectivity as possible. In addition to numerous barcharts, time series, and figures presenting his own and public data on the
political and sociological characteristics of the city, Dahl documented specific procedures for the construction of social indices and the evaluation of elite interviews
(these were tucked demurely in a methodological appendix at the end of the book, another procedure typical of the time, an apparent effort not to appear offensively behavioral). These three characteristics are in accord with behavioralism as it wished

to perceive itself: innovative, broadly open to alternative approaches to politics, and thoroughly based on carefully collected empirical foundations.

The overall structure of *Who Governs?* illustrates also a typical behavioralist pattern of combining an explicitly objective research study with an implicit normative agenda. The first four sections of the book are straightforward description, political and sociological, of politics in New Haven, emphasizing the inequalities, the sources and range of the inequalities between participants, the several patterns of elite rule, and so on. The final chapter contrasts rather interestingly with the earlier ones. The reader, while prepared to allow an author great liberty with the final chapter of a long work, perhaps expected a conclusion that would gather the empirical findings into some coherent if preliminary theory about who governs in local politics and perhaps beyond. Instead, in *Who Governs?* the reader finds a discussion of democracy and its stability and feels that somehow this is a different book from the empirical one.

What in New Haven's rather plodding history could lead to discussion of the risks of democracy and of ignorant people being "deceived by appeals intended to destroy democracy in the name of democracy" (Dahl, 1961, p. 325)? This concluding attack of anxiety suggests that the major uncited source in *Who Governs?* is Karl Marx, who did predict that economic interests would control government, and to whose predictions New Haven did not provide a fully robust refutation. If a behavioralist wanted to join in Cold War debates, that was any man's prerogative and it should not be denied to him. The problem was that often ideological questions were used to conclude a research work, rather than the authors' undertaking the more necessary, and more difficult, task of figuring out the concrete theoretical results of their research. In later years, when behavioralism would run out of steam, this failure to face hard facts and conceptual challenges would be high on the list of reasons.

THE SPOKESMAN OF THE REVOLUTION

It is impossible to discuss the behavioral revolution in political science without including reference to the writings of David Easton, who early became the revolution's spokesman and whose books on the "political system" became central texts of the behavioral movement (Easton, 1953, 1965a, 1965b). But the subject is a complicated one, and the precise nature of Easton's contribution to the discipline is not easy to pin down. As the bellwether of the changes in political science at the period after World War II, Easton once again made plain the truth that it is easy to criticize the past, but exceptionally difficult to define the future. In criticizing earlier forms of political science, Easton's work was accorded the liveliest approval his colleagues in the discipline could bestow. In developing his alternative general theory, however, he took a direction very few would choose to follow. But his endeavors to turn the discipline can tell the inquirer much about the behavioral revolution and the discipline it so agitated, for good or ill.

In Easton's first book (1953) he advanced the suggestion, with which so many of his colleagues in the discipline heartily agreed, that the results of 2500 years of political science were disappointing. Political science, he argued, could not clearly define its terms, nor know what kinds of data were relevant. The solution was scientific method, he said, which would allow in-depth examination of political processes. Easton placed great emphasis on the role of political theory, which he felt had been debased by being treated in a historical sense rather than as the center of a living research-oriented discipline. His central objective was to move the discipline beyond its emphasis on everyday "politicking" toward a concern with system-wide policy; this purpose was expressed in his well-known definition of politics as "the authoritative allocation of values for a society" (Easton, 1953, p. 128).

Easton's second and third books, both published in 1965 and forming a single manuscript,[18] began the attempt to construct a theory that would serve as a master plan for integrating the political science discipline and directing research to the important rather than the trivial aspects of the political system—thus building toward a true science of politics. The systems theory Easton developed in the two works is easy to summarize because Easton abstracted its elements to such high conceptual levels that there was nothing much left of it. Easton's own diagram of the political system is a black box labeled "the political system" with arrows marked "input" going in, arrows marked "output" coming out, and the whole resting in an "environment" through which a feedback loop connected governmental outputs to citizens' inputs. The question at the center of Easton's attention constantly recurs: "How do . . . systems manage to persist" in the face of environmental stress, or what are the "fundamental functions without which no system could endure" (Easton, 1965b, p. 17)? The central metaphor was a system under constant stress from the environment ("demands") struggling to make policy, held together by the loyalty ("support") of the members.

BEHAVIORALISM AND SYSTEMS THEORY

Easton's theory has been much discussed in the literature: He was criticized for the level of abstraction that seemed to achieve universality of application to all sorts of tribes and nations only by being quite empty of content or explanatory power; he was attacked for his overuse of the concept of equilibrium, which seemed impossible to define in any coherent way; he was pilloried for combining inconsistent concepts, particularly both a micro- and a macro-analytic viewpoint, within the same theory. Tacit recognition of these problems was given by Easton's fourth book on general theory, which appeared over twenty years after the others, and continued to pursue the same unsettled issues (1990). Nonetheless, Easton holds a unique position within political science, as perhaps the only man who ever attempted a fully unified theory of politics, and there are important lessons to be learned from his body of work.

First, Easton's program exemplifies a recognition that if political science was to be objective, and especially of concern here if it was to be at all comparative, there was an inescapable necessity to find analytic categories that would be appropriate to diverse situations. Clearly "democracy" would not fill this need. Easton himself frequently refers to various primitive societies, to small groups, traditional societies, as well as advanced industrial nations as examples. "Demands," "stress," and "support" did not seem to the discipline of political science to be sufficient to the task set for them. But the goal itself was entirely correct, if perhaps premature.

A second lesson is the impetus given by Easton's systems approach to the enlargement of the subject matter of political science. While Easton's treatment sometimes waffles between using the "political system" as a synonym for "government" and using it as an inclusive term involving everything at the grassroots as well, he settles on using the political system in its largest sense, and this became a part of political language. Even if the term was used in a casual sense, without thinking of its implications, the existence of "the political system" as a handy term for what political scientists study, made a permanent mark, and always contained at least the possibility that everyone, official and unofficial alike, was part of the discipline's purview. Even though this approach led to the later criticism that Easton had "eliminated" the state, dissolving it into a mere vehicle for social forces, the change was progressive.

Thirdly, Easton's work reflected the ambivalence common to the behavioral revolution about just what is the best way to run a democracy. Do we want sharp, active, participating citizens? or would it be easier if the citizens were docile, tractable, loyal, and tolerant of the government's failures? Easton's answer is only implicit, but it is clear in the very organization of his work, where long initial chapters are devoted to "support," especially the diffuse support that citizens give on symbolic patriotic grounds, before he even reaches the topic one might have expected to be discussed much earlier—the actual government response to actual citizen demands.

BEHAVIORALISM AND ITS "CREED"

To conclude this chapter on revolutions and the very strange bedfellows they create, it is appropriate to consider Easton's "definition" of behavioralism, which has been so often quoted that it has become virtually the "official" definition of the movement. In reading its short list of precepts it is useful to bear in mind the various examples of behavioral classics discussed so far in this chapter, and to wonder how well the definition covers their motley variety.

> *1. Regularities. There are discoverable uniformities in political behavior. These can be expressed in generalizations or theories with explanatory or predictive value.*
> *2. Verification. The validity of such generalizations must be treatable, in principle, by reference to relevant behavior.*
> *3. Techniques. Means for acquiring and interpreting data . . . are problematic and need to be examined self-consciously, refined, and validated. . . .*

*4. Quantification. Precision in the recording of data and the statement of
findings requires measurement and quantification . . . where possible, relevant, and meaningful in the light of other objectives.
5. Values. Ethical evaluation and empirical explanation . . . should be kept
analytically distinct.
6. Systematization. . . . theory and research are to be seen as closely intertwined parts of a coherent and orderly body of knowledge. . . .
7. Pure science . . . the understanding and explanation of political behavior
logically precede and provide the basis for efforts to utilize political knowledge. . . .
8. Integration. . . . political research can ignore the findings of other disci-
plines (in the social sciences) only at the peril of weakening the validity and
undermining the generality of its own results (Easton, 1965a, p. 7).*

In retrospect, it may seem that this list of defining characteristics has had less influence on the research that actually defined the behavioral revolution than it did on
the debate over behavioralism. By the 1970s if not before, the debate had degenerated
into two opposing parties who threw strawman arguments past each other, wasting
time on polemics (which are easy and fun) that should have been spent on clarifying
concepts and theories and proceeding with meaningful research (which is difficult
and usually not fun). Political scientists, like politicians, often enjoy a good fight for
its own sake, quite ignoring its possible costs in terms of opportunities lost. Comparativists, facing a world that everywhere challenges their understanding, were less
prone to futile battles and more committed to deeper research questions, than many
of their brethren. But that is another chapter.

NOTES

1. Histories of political science as a discipline took on a greater interest as a result of the
behavioral movement. The most widely known of these histories (Somit and Tanenhaus, 1967)
began with "prehistory," defined as before 1880, and moved in twenty-year increments to the
behavioralist period, which it called "easily the paramount development in the discipline's entire history" (Somit and Tanenhaus, 1967, p. 173). A footnote lists a score of political scientists
involved in the "controversy" over behavioralism from both the positive and negative points of
view (Somit and Tanenhaus, 1967, pp. 173–174).

2. Edited collections of articles on different approaches within the behavioral movement
that can still be consulted today to catch the flavor of the time include Eulau's *Political Behavior in America: New Directions* (1966); Polsby, Dentler, and Smith's *Politics and Social Life:
An Introduction to Political Behavior* (1963); and Ulmer's *Introductory Readings in Political
Behavior* (1961).

3. The search for "empirical theory" took many directions. Some pursued theory relevant to democratic systems (Kariel, 1970); others studied contributions from other social sciences such as history, anthropology, and economics (Lipset, 1969); others viewed current

issues in terms of the traditional fields, such as public policy (Pool, 1967); still others sought (for perhaps the last time) to integrate traditional political theory with its more modern varieties (Dahl and Neubauer, 1968).

4. For similar criticisms see Easton's *The Political System* (1953).

5. The immense expansion of the ICPSR archives is documented in current catalogs, which run to several hundred pages and include data sets from throughout the world.

6. Similarly distressing results in respect to the American electorate were presented in Stouffer's study of attitudes during the early Cold War period, where mass respondents were found frequently to deny civil liberties to "deviants" of all sorts (Stouffer, 1963, pp. 26–57). For an alternative approach to American voters see Lane (1962).

7. Serious methodological issues involving the analysis of political data have been raised by Achen (1983), who complains that "several decades after its beginning, political methodology has so far failed to make serious theoretical progress on any of the major issues facing it" (Achen, 1983, p. 69), primarily measurement error and aggregation bias.

8. Methodology texts in comparative politics during the behavioral period ranged widely over quantitative and qualitative approaches. Representative works included Holt and Turner (1970), Bill and Hardgrave (1973), Scarrow (1969), and Merritt and Rokkan (1966). A comprehensive collection edited by Eckstein and Apter (1963) presented materials on constitutional government, electoral systems, political parties and interest groups, totalitarianism, political change and political development; along with analytic essays by the editors that sought to provide perspective on recent comparative work.

9. The quotation is from the original 1963 hardback edition of *The Civic Culture,* p. 76; the passage does not occur in the paperback edition. All citations in this section are to the hardback edition.

10. A major exponent of the national character approach was Geoffrey Gorer, who wrote studies of the English, Russian, and American characters in the 1950s and 1960s. Strong traces of the style can still be found, frequently among journalists who have been stationed abroad; a fine example is Bernstein (1991) on the French.

11. This division into cognitive, affective, and evaluative aspects of culture was typical of the sociological literature of the period; see, for instance, Parsons and Shils (1951).

12. A recent analysis of the Italian political system restores the balance (LaPalombara, 1987). The work is particularly interesting because of the author's former close association with structural functionalism (see his contribution to Binder, 1971).

13. Discussions of Merriam and the Chicago School can be found in Karl (1974), Tsou (1955), Seidelman (1985, pp. 111–131), and Gabriel Almond's oral interview included in Baer, Jewell, and Sigelman (1991, pp. 121–134).

14. Other works that constituted the "founding generation" in rational choice theory included Simon (1965), Buchanan and Tullock (1965), Riker (1962), and Schelling (1963).

15. When the issue arose in comparative politics as to what were the defining criteria of "theory," scholars frequently adopted the model presented by rational choice theory, even if they did not themselves adhere to the school; see, for instance, Holt and Turner's (1975) rejection of the crisis sequence model.

16. In the aftermath of the Second World War, studies of the "authoritarian personality," that is, the fascist personality, had considerable interest. The methods used in these studies were later criticized for biases that were said to distort the authoritarian qualities (Adorno, Frenkel-Brunswik, Levinson, and Sanford, 1950).

17. These elite studies were dominated by the work of Floyd Hunter's work in Atlanta (1953), and employed a "reputational" method that based conclusions about elite rule on citizens' opinions about whether such elites existed. In the political science literature, in addition to Dahl's study, see Polsby et al. (1963).

18. That the two works were only split to meet the requests of publishers was not fully understood at the time; Easton discusses it in the oral history edited by Baer, Jewell, and Sigelman (1991).

REFERENCES

Achen, Christopher H. "Toward Theories of Data: The State of Political Methodology." In Ada W. Finifter. (Ed.). *Political Science: The State of the Discipline* (pp. 69–93). Washington, D.C.: American Political Science Association, 1983.

Adorno, T. W., Else Frenkel-Brunswik, Daniel Levinson, and R. Nevitt Sanford. *The Authoritarian Personality*. New York: Norton, 1950.

Almond, Gabriel A., and Sidney Verba. *The Civic Culture*. Princeton: Princeton University Press, 1963.

Almond, Gabriel A., and Sidney Verba (Eds.) *The Civic Culture Revisited*. Boston: Little Brown, 1980.

Baer, Michael A., Malcolm E. Jewell, and Lee Sigelman (Eds.) *Political Science in America: Oral Histories of a Discipline*. Lexington: University of Kentucky, 1991.

Bernstein, Richard. *Fragile Glory: A Portrait of France and of the French*. New York: Penguin, 1991.

Bill, James A., and Robert L. Hardgrave, Jr. *Comparative Politics: The Quest for Theory*. Columbus: Merrill, 1973.

Binder, Leonard et al. *Crisis and Sequences in Political Development*. Princeton: Princeton University Press, 1971.

Buchanan, James M., and Gordon Tullock. *The Calculus of Consent* (1962). Ann Arbor: University of Michigan Press, 1965.

Campbell, Angus, Philip E. Converse, Warren E. Miller, and Donald E. Stokes. *The American Voter* (1960). New York: Wiley, 1964.

Dahl, Robert A. *Who Governs? Democracy and Power in an American City*. New Haven: Yale University Press, 1961.

Dahl, Robert A., and Deane E. Neubauer (Eds.). *Readings in Modern Political Analysis*. Englewood Cliffs: Prentice Hall, 1968.

Downs, Anthony. *An Economic Theory of Democracy*. New York: Harper and Row, 1957.

Easton, David. *The Political System: An Inquiry into the State of Political Science*. New York: Alfred A. Knopf, 1953.

Easton, David. *A Framework for Political Analysis*. Englewood Cliffs: Prentice Hall, 1965a.

Easton, David. *A Systems Analysis of Political Life*. New York: John Wiley and Sons, 1965b.

Easton, David. *The Analysis Of Political Structure*. New York: Routledge, 1990.

Eckstein, Harry, and David E. Apter (Eds.). *Comparative Politics: A Reader*. New York: The Free Press of Glencoe, 1963.

Eulau, Heinz, Samuel J. Eldersveld, and Morris Janowitz (Eds.). *Political Behavior: A Reader in Theory and Research*. Glencoe: Free Press, 1956.

Eulau, Heinz (Ed.). *Political Behavior in America: New Directions*. New York: Random House, 1966.

Holt, Robert T., and John E. Turner (Eds.). *The Methodology of Comparative Research*. New York: The Free Press, 1970.

Holt, Robert T., and John E. Turner. "Crises and Sequences in Collective Theory Development." *American Political Science Review* LXIX no. 3 (September 1975): 979–94.

Hunter, Floyd. *Community Power Structure: A Study of Decision Makers*. Chapel Hill: University of North Carolina Press, 1953.

Kariel, Henry S. (Ed.). *Frontiers of Democratic Theory*. New York: Random House, 1970.

Karl, Barry D. *Charles E. Merriam and the Study of Politics*. Chicago: University of Chicago Press, 1974.

Lane, Robert E. *Political Ideology: Why the American Common Man Believes What He Does*. New York: Free Press of Glencoe, 1962.

LaPalombara, Joseph. *Democracy, Italian Style*. New Haven: Yale University Press, 1987.

Lasswell, Harold D. *Psychopathology and Politics*. Chicago: University of Chicago Press, 1930.

Lasswell, Harold D., and Abraham Kaplan. *Power and Society: A Framework for Political Inquiry*. New Haven: Yale University Press, 1950.

Lazarsfeld, Paul F., Bernard Berelson, and Hazel Gaudet. *The People's Choice*. New York: Columbia University Press, 1968.

Lipset, Seymour Martin. *Political Man: The Social Bases of Politics*. New York: Anchor Books, 1963 (1960).

Lipset, Seymour Martin (Ed.). *Politics and the Social Sciences*. New York: Oxford University Press, 1969.

Lipset, Seymour Martin, Martin A. Trow, and James Smoot Coleman. *Union Democracy: The Internal Politics of the International Typographical Union*. Glencoe: Free Press, 1956.

Lynd, Robert, and Helen Lynd. *Middletown: A Study in Contemporary American Culture*. New York: Harcourt Brace, 1929.

Macridis, Roy C. *The Study of Comparative Government*. New York: Random House, 1955.

Merritt, Richard L., and Stein Rokkan. (Eds.). *Comparing Nations: The Use of Quantitative Data in Cross-National Research*. New Haven: Yale University Press, 1966.

Nelson, Joan M. "Political Participation." In Myron Weiner and Samuel P. Huntington (Eds). *Understanding Political Development* (pp. 103–59). Glenview: Little Brown, 1987.

Parsons, Talcott, and Edward A. Shils (Eds.). *Toward a General Theory of Action: Theoretical Foundations for the Social Sciences*. Cambridge: Harvard, 1951. (Harper Torchbooks, 1962.)

Polsby, Nelson W., Robert A. Dentler, and Paul A. Smith. *Politics and Social Life: An Introduction to Political Behavior*. Boston: Houghton Mifflin, 1963.

Pool, Ithiel de Sola. (Ed.). *Contemporary Political Science: Toward Empirical Theory*. New York: McGraw Hill, 1967.

Pye, Lucien W., and Sidney Verba (Eds.). *Political Culture and Political Development*. Princeton: Princeton University Press, 1965.

Ricci, David M. *The Tragedy of Political Science: Scholarship, and Democracy*. New Haven: Yale, 1984.

Riker, William H. *The Theory of Political Coalitions*. New Haven: Yale University Press, 1962.

Scarrow, Howard A. *Comparative Political Analysis: An Introduction*. New York: Harper and Row, 1969.

Schelling, Thomas. *Strategy of Conflict*. New York: Oxford Galaxy, 1963.

Seidelman, Raymond, with Edward J. Harpham. *Disenchanted Realists: Political Science and the American Crisis 1884–1984*. Albany: SUNY Press, 1985.

Simon, Herbert A. *Administrative Behavior: A Study of Decision-Making Process in Administrative Organization* (1945). New York: Free Press, 1965.

Somit, Albert, and Joseph Tanenhaus. *The Development of Political Science*. Boston: Allyn and Bacon, 1967.

Stouffer, Samuel A. *Communism, Conformity, and Civil Liberties: A Cross-section of the Nation Speaks Its Mind*. Gloucester: Peter Smith, 1963.

Tsou, Tang. "Fact and Value in Charles E. Merriam." *Southwestern Social Science Quarterly* 36, no. 1 (June 1955): 9–26.

Ulmer, S. Sidney (Ed.). *Introductory Readings In Political Behavior*. Chicago: Rand McNally, 1961.

Warner, W. Lloyd (Ed.). *Yankee City* (One volume, abridged edition). New Haven: Yale University Press, 1963.

Political Development, Its Rise, Decline, and Transformation

In comparative politics, as in many things, necessity has been the mother of invention, and political events have been a primary stimulus in the development of new theoretic approaches, concepts, and research concerns. This pattern is as old as Hobbes, who said he constructed his Leviathan upon the fear stimulated by the Spanish Armada's assault on England; or as new as Weimar Germany, when political scientists discovered that an excellent democratic constitution will not alone correct a nation's political problems. The development literature illustrates the same point. The changes in the international political system during and after the second world war, the emergence of new nations and the resuscitation of others, presented comparative politics with new political situations and the new challenges that followed from them. No longer could the field define itself upon concepts appropriate to the "major foreign powers" of Europe; a "new" world seemed to emerge, and left comparativists scrambling to catch up with its possibilities.[1]

The inquiry went through several stages, at first a peculiarly American optimism that the new nations with the least bit of friendly help would blossom into smaller versions of ourselves, and at length the discovery that this prospect was massively false, and that states might go backwards, or go nowhere, rather than progressing. This was the practical problem. It was accompanied by a not entirely parallel theoretical problem of finding conceptual frameworks that might assist in the management of the awesome diversity of experience represented by the world's many political systems. Political scientists specializing in the American political system can easily ignore theoretical problems, because there is so much data so openly available on so many levels of government, that in the United States the sheer collection of facts can keep one usefully occupied for several lifetimes. Theory is, however, crucial to comparativists, who encounter challenges to all their assumptions, biases, and preconceptions as soon as they leave the comfortable security of their native lands.

This was among the reasons why comparativists played a major role in the behavioral revolution, and why their theoretical struggles have continued longer and more successfully than those in less difficult areas of study. But if development theory begins naively, it grows over the years and becomes wiser as it turns into a more general theory of institutionalization and change. Many of its discoveries were present even in the early years of the behavioral period, but it took several decades to separate the conceptual wheat from the chaff.

POLITICAL SCIENCE IN A TURKISH VILLAGE

Thirty years after the first writings in political development appeared, it is difficult to explain the boundless optimism shared by participants and observers alike as new nations shook off the various chains of poverty, tradition, and colonialism. The flavor of the time is well represented by Daniel Lerner's early work, *The Passing of Traditional Society* (1958), which reflected and reinforced many people's ideas about the development process. One picture is worth many words, and it is possible to think ourselves back into the attitudes of the time by considering the picture Lerner painted of the town of Balgat, just outside the capital of Ankara, Turkey.

Readers of Lerner's study first meet the village through the eyes of a young Turkish student who interviewed the inhabitants in 1950. Tosun B. was particularly depressed by the place: The village is barren, he wrote, everything is gray and dusty and it is a shapeless dump. Although it is only 8 miles south of Ankara, the roads are so bad that it takes two hours to get there (Lerner, 1958, pp. 19–20). The chief of the village was interviewed and did not have answers to most of the questions, but was emphatic on "modes of human deportment." His sons, said the chief, needed to know only how to fight as bravely as their fathers, and how to die. Asked what he would do if he was president of Turkey, the chief said he could barely manage the village, let alone the nation (Lerner, 1958, pp. 22–23).

The other major character in the village was the grocer, and he was a complete contrast to the chief. Asked what he would do as president of Turkey he had a list of specific ideas about better roads and other improvements. Asked where he would like to live if he had to leave Turkey (most respondents could not imagine this, and said they would rather die), the grocer instantly said, "America . . . a nice country, and with possibilities to be rich even for the simplest persons" (Lerner, 1958, pp. 23–25).

Balgat's significance for comparative politics was established not by its initial dusty introduction to the world, but by its subsequent changes. When Lerner visited the village four years after the initial interviews were done, he found change everywhere. There was a new road, so the trip only took a half hour; the village had been electrified and pure water was piped in from a new well. New buildings were everywhere; instead of the former fifty buildings there were now 500, and the chief said he no longer knew the people he met on the streets. There was a new headquarters of the metropolitan police in the village, regular bus service (huge Mercedes models), and there were virtually no farm laborers left, for all now worked in Ankara. Where once only the chief had a radio, and all the village came by daily to sit and listen, now there were 100 receivers (Lerner, 1958, pp. 30–34).

When asked how this all came about, villagers said it began with the 1950 election. When the opposition Demokrat Party visited the village and promised if elected to make all these changes, the village voted for them, they won, and they carried out their promises (Lerner, 1958, p. 30). Thus the glorious alliance of democracy and modernization.

PAINLESS, AUTOMATIC DEVELOPMENT

The tale seemed to speak for itself. There were progressive forces everywhere, along with the backward ones, and democracy and a modern market orientation would sweep everyone easily forward into a glorious future. No one seemed to ask, at the time, whether economic development had been so simple for the early modernizing states of Europe and North America, whether their experience gave any grounds for believing modernization could come so smoothly. Instead the rising optimism lifted all hearts. This approach to development was expressed in Rostow's immensely popular theory of the stages of economic development (1960, pp. 4–12).

1. The stage of traditional society, which was characterized by pre-Newtonian thought, science, and technology; and was predominantly agricultural. "The central fact about the traditional society was that a ceiling existed on the level of attainable output per head." The population was at the mercy of plague and war, and had attitudes of "long run" fatalism (Rostow, 1960, pp. 4–5).

2. The stage of preconditions, characterized by technological advances from within or outside the country. "The idea spreads not merely that economic progress is possible, but that economic progress is a necessary condition for some other purpose, judged to be good: be it national dignity, private profit, the general welfare, or a better life for the children" (Rostow, 1960, p. 6).

3. The stage of "take off," where the resistance to economic growth disappears, agriculture is commercialized, industry and investment expand, income increases, the entrepreneurial class expands, and new technologies spread (Rostow, 1960, p. 8).

4. The "drive toward maturity" where production regularly exceeds population growth. It is "the stage in which an economy demonstrates the capacity to move beyond the original industries which powered its take-off and to absorb and to apply efficiently over a very wide range of its resources . . . the most advanced fruits of (then) modern technology" (Rostow, 1960, p. 10).

5. The age of high mass consumption, where leading sectors of the economy shift toward consumer goods and services, and "where a large number of persons gained a command over consumption which transcended basic food, shelter, and clothing"; the stage included increased urbanization and factory employment (Rostow, 1960, p. 10).

6. "The search for quality" stage, characterized by concern to enrich private lives in conditions of abundance (this stage was added in 1971 by Rostow).

THEORY OF THE "DEVELOPING" NATIONS

A more theoretical approach to issues of national development was taken in a work that by its title summarized the discipline that was to come; yet its basic assumptions were not necessarily more realistic. *The Politics of the Developing Areas* (Almond and Coleman, 1960) gave the new nations an optimistic name and a new theory, structural-functionalism, which would for fifteen years represent the hoped-for promised land of comparative theory.[2] The aura of Balgat remained in the air.

"Structural-functionalism" always puzzles newcomers to the field of comparative politics; indeed, it sometimes puzzles old hands as well. There is not only the seven-syllable name to contend with, but the problem of what the name might mean, given that structuralism and functionalism are often seen as two different theories. For the comparative political scientist, the easiest method of approach is by considering structural-functionalism as an example of the diffusion and modification of ideas. Once one has gotten rid of the notion that ideas or concepts are universal, absolute, and given in the nature of rational intelligence (and the practice of comparative politics very quickly relieves anyone of this notion), then the question is, Where do ideas come from? The most immediate answer in respect to the origin of conceptual frameworks in any discipline is that they are begged, borrowed, or stolen from elsewhere. Such was the case with structural-functionalism. The flavor of the theory came from anthropology and sociology, the name came from Talcott Parsons, who employed it in his translations of the work of Max Weber, and in reference to his own social theory.[3]

Structural-functionalism in political science is best classified as a form of functionalism, although it should be understood that it is a form peculiar to political science and not necessarily closely tied to functionalism in other social sciences. Functionalism was initially thought to be the solution to the whole problem of the macro-social sciences because by postulating that every social system had the same basic needs, functionalism provided the basis for truly cross-national research. One did not have to attempt to compare, say, Chinese warlords with British Members of Parliament and despair of finding any institutions common between them on which a comparison could be based. Instead, by using the idea that all societies have the same functional requisites, warlords and Members of Parliament could be compared not on the basis of their very different institutional arrangements, but on the common functions they might serve.[4]

The meaning of "function" is in certain cases perfectly clear. For a human being, for instance, there is the necessity that blood move through the circulatory system to provide nutrients and other substances to the cells; without this circulation the organism dies. Nutrition is therefore "a need that must somehow be met if the organism is to survive." Such a need is a "functional necessity," and anything that meets that need serves that function for the organism.

However, the problem in social and political science was more difficult. It was to determine what such universal functions might be, for a social or a political system, where "need" does not mean the same as it does in biological systems, and where the meaning of life and death are not anywhere so clear. The challenge led to some truly creative thinking at very high levels of abstraction. Parsons defined four functions for his social system: adaptation, integration, pattern maintenance, and goal attainment (Parsons, 1951). Anthropologists proposed longer lists: the provision for food and maintenance of membership levels, role differentiation and assignment, linguistic symbols for shared communication, shared cognitive orientations, the control of disruptive behavior, and so on (Aberle, Cohen, Davis, Levy, and Sutton, 1950). Other functional traditions within sociology preferred to avoid the grander issues entirely, and worked with middle-level functions (Merton, 1957).

THE SEARCH FOR FUNCTIONS

The branch of structural-functional theory associated with several books co-authored by Gabriel Almond cut the Gordian knot by inventing its own set of specifically political functions. The definition of these political functions illustrates how idea systems become modified, and where the new elements come from; it also speaks to the perils of endeavoring to think "objectively," and the way in which old habits will intrude on apparently new thoughts. Almond and Coleman (1960) originally defined four input and three output functions, arguing that these same functions are characteristic of all political systems—even the simplest—and that systems could be compared according to the type and specialization of the structures that fulfilled the functions (this was where the "structural" entered structural-functionalism). The input functions were postulated as interest articulation, interest aggregation, communication, and socialization; the output functions as rule making, rule execution, and rule adjudication. (Almond and Coleman, 1960, p. 17). Especially illustrative of the problem of cultural parochialism inherent in the items in this list are the output functions, which are clearly based on the three branches of the American government—the legislative, the executive, and the judicial branches.[5]

That the U.S. political system was being used tacitly as the model for all other political systems in Almond's version of structural-functionalism became even more plain in the textbook series in comparative politics edited by Almond and Powell, where structural-functionalism is directly linked to the "separation of powers" theory of the American constitution. If the goal of functionalism was to provide a more comprehensive scope for comparative research and to break out of the traditional western political categories, as Almond and Powell argued (1966, p. 6), then the use of

categories so closely tied to the U. S. experience was hazardous at best. Many theorists, notably Samuel Huntington, have argued that in fact the United States was, and
is, an anomaly in history and therefore particularly unsuited for use as a general
model (see below).

POLITICAL DEVELOPMENT AND CRISIS THEORY

Another branch of structural-functional inquiry took a different direction from the
separation of powers approach. This second body of inquiry was incorporated in a series of books, all sponsored by the Social Science Research Council's Committee on
Comparative Politics, published in the years between 1963 and 1978, exploring different aspects of political development, such as political communications, the bureaucracy, education, political culture, and political parties.[6] The series culminated,
from the point of view of theory development, in a 1971 volume edited by Leonard
Binder that endeavored to draw together the earlier studies under the heading of a
"crises and sequences" theory of political development, including chapters by James
Coleman, Lucien Pye, Myron Weiner, Joseph LaPalombara, and Sidney Verba, all of
whom had made and would continue to make major contributions in other areas of
comparative politics.[7]

Coleman's chapter defined political development in terms of three concepts as "a
continuous interaction among the processes of structural *differentiation,* the imperatives of *equality,* and the integrative, responsive and adaptive *capacity* of a political
system.

> *Political development, in these terms, is seen as the acquisition by a politi-
> cal system of a consciously sought, and a qualitatively new and enhanced
> political capacity as manifested in the successful institutionalization of (1)
> new patterns of integration and penetration regulating and containing the
> tensions and conflicts produced by increased differentiation, and (2) new
> patterns of participation and resource distribution adequately responsive to
> the demands generated by the imperatives of equality. The acquisition of
> such a performance capacity is, in turn, a decisive factor in the resolution of
> the problems of identity and legitimacy. (Coleman, 1971, pp. 74–75)*

Each of the emphasized terms was seen as the basis for a potential crisis of development, junctures at which conflicting tensions would either be resolved (functionally
satisfied) or the system would stop or regress. The general theoretical hypothesis underlying the work was that the crises would occur in a particular sequence in all political systems; this failed in every test to which it was put.[8]

The Binder volume did, however, contain much that was of interest; in many
cases this was because the contributors did not use the structural framework alone but
supplemented it with the microanalytics of group behavior. Pye presented the discus-

sion of identity and legitimacy crises, which were said to occur when citizens questioned, respectively, the basic unity of the political group or the proprieties of government. Leaving behind the grand functional categories, Pye emphasized the importance in the two crises of the role taken by the governing elite: whether the elites were willing to open their ranks and allow new members of the society access to benefits, or whether they shut out some groups and classes and kept the benefits to themselves. For identity and legitimacy Pye substituted their opposite, alienation, as a major component of the analysis.

Myron Weiner's analysis of the participation crisis also emphasized the importance of elite-mass interactions, and suggested that meaningful participation required the prior development of an informed citizenry, and that if democratic institutions were imposed from the top down, the desired result was unlikely to occur. Crises of participation, Weiner argued, were not one-time-only events, like identity and legitimacy crises, but would recur any time social or economic change produced newly active groups that sought to take part in political procedures. The crises of penetration and distribution discussed by LaPalombara both related to system capacity and reflected the concerns of an older political science—How does the government get its citizens to obey its directives?[9]

CRITICISM OF STRUCTURAL-FUNCTIONALISM

The crisis and sequence branch of structural-functionalism met an abrupt end for three reasons. First, it was challenged by the final two volumes in the series, which were edited by historians and suggested that the theory was not even appropriate to the European pattern of development, much less to the developing world (Tilly, 1975; Grew, 1978). The second challenge came from within, in a critical chapter by Sidney Verba that concluded the Binder volume and suggested that the conceptual framework was so loose as to border on the meaningless (Verba, 1971). This theme was taken up in the third attack on crisis-sequence theory, a devastating critique published in the most prestigious of the political science journals, the *American Political Science Review* (Holt and Turner, 1975) in which the authors argued that the theory contained in the Binder volume could not rigorously be defined as a theory at all, that what passed for a theory (the sequence of crises) was demonstrably wrong, and that much of the problem should have been obvious at the start of the project. In fact, they remarked, it might be said that "seventeen years of prodigious effort" had come to nothing (Holt and Turner, 1975, p. 988).

While there was in the historical record some support for these charges, they are more important for our present purposes in what they revealed about comparative politics as a field—a tendency to adopt theories somewhat uncritically, and to expect these theories to solve all the discipline's problems at a single stroke. A further problem is that there is in comparative politics, as in political science as a whole, considerable doubt about just what a theory is.[10] This ambiguity was further demonstrated by the uncertain position of another classic in the development literature of the period, which was of major importance but did not fit neatly into any available methodological category.

DEVELOPMENT AND POLITICAL ORDER

Samuel Huntington is one of the best known political scientists in the field of comparative politics, and his book on development is one of the best known works, but it has not always been clear how Huntington's approach should be classified. *Political Order in Changing Societies* (Huntington, 1968) is famous for its harsh conclusions about the possibilities and processes of political development, most especially for Huntington's conviction that development might not be semiautomatic as the structural-functionalists originally believed.

In addition, the reader of the book is struck by the author's conviction that development requires the building of old-fashioned political power, and that, in their recognition of this, nobody beat communist parties. In later years when the original development theorists had been forced to learn some hard lessons about the process of development, Huntington's book was welcomed as evidence that structural-functionalism had never ignored the state. But in the early days, Huntington worked outside the mainstream, although the vigor of his ideas brought him many readers.

An example of the way in which Huntington's arguments placed him in a unique position within the discipline is his analysis of the political institutions of the United States. While most developmentalists assumed without question that the American political system was close enough to some democratic ideal that it could be used as a model for the rest of the world and for analytic political science, Huntington argued the contrary thesis. If political modernization has three aspects, Huntington said, the rationalization of authority, the differentiation of structures, and the expansion of participation, then the United States is foremost only in participation, while lacking in rationalization and differentiation. The modern state in Europe, according to Huntington, developed through a process of gradual replacement of feudal institutions: The church was subordinated, then the medieval estates were suppressed, the aristocracy was weakened, the state bureaucracy and public services were rationalized, standing armies were created and expanded, and taxation extended (Huntington, 1968, p. 95).

But instead of waiting until this centralizing process was complete, Huntington argued, the American colonists took off for the new world bearing with them political ideas based on an already outdated sixteenth century Tudor constitution, which retained many medieval ideas that became embedded in the U.S. political experience. A list of these "medieval" qualities supports Huntington's argument, for all are recognizably typical of the American system: the idea of an organic union of society and government, the harmony of authorities within the government, the subordination of government to fundamental law, the intermingling of the legal and political realms, the balance of power between crown and parliament, the complementary representative roles of those two bodies, the vitality of local governments, and a reliance on militia for defense (Huntington, 1968, p. 96).

The difference between the European and American experience is easy to explain, Huntington said, because in the United States there were none of the "enemies" (the feudal order and the aristocracy) against which the European state had been created. Modernization in the United States was so effortless, so unimpeded, according to Huntington, that strong political institutions were never needed and were not created. So while *economic* development is strong in the United States, the country's *political* modernization is "attenuated and incomplete" and the U.S. political system is an anachronism in the modern world, a Tudor leftover. The United States has little therefore to offer modernizing nations, Huntington concluded, because it never modernized but was born modern. The Kremlin, he added, would be a more appropriate model for the developing world (Huntington, 1968, p. 135). While Huntington would, many years later, take up "democratization" theory, he has never excelled the chastening originality of this early work.

THE THEORIES OF PRAETORIANISM

The central theoretical concept in *Political Order in Changing Societies* is praetorianism. In its narrow sense, praetorianism means the intervention of the military in politics, an event of obvious relevance to occurrences in many Third World nations. Some political scientists consider Huntington's major contribution to be, in fact, his attention to soldiers in politics. But Huntington gives praetorianism an expanded meaning, one that makes it a general term for the presence of, and conflict between, any social groups without the mediation of political institutions of some kind. Here praetorianism is an element in Huntington's general theory of institutionalization.

Critics have in recent years argued that any written text has no single meaning but is open to multiple interpretations. This is certainly the case with Huntington's *Political Order,* which was initially interpreted as a set of opinions about development, rather than as systematic theory. More recently Huntington's work has been adopted as a precursor of the "return to the state" because of its emphasis on institutions; here also his theory, as distinct from his substantive focus, is ignored. Yet in a recent book Huntington himself says that the object of the book was the building of universal theory (Huntington, 1991, p. xv). One begins to wonder why his theoretical contribution has been so often ignored.

The tendency to overlook the theoretical aspects of *Political Order in Changing Society* arises from the type of theory involved, a sort of embedded logic that does not clothe itself in abstract categories (systems, functions, or equilibria) but works deductively from within the events it analyzes. Many political scientists applaud deductive theory when it is used in the field of political economy, tracing the ways in which economic men may all benefit from the exchanges in the marketplace. Deductive theory has traditionally been less well received when it is advanced by Machiavelli rather than by Adam Smith, and when it suggests that in the political marketplace like-minded individuals may end up cutting one another's throats. Objections to such conclusions seem to have led to a disdain for the method.

Huntington, quite in line with Machiavelli, whom he frequently quotes, assumes that people have a capacity for vicious behavior and that in unstable political circumstances (like the underdeveloped world) everyone may be grimly self-interested, and that even those who are not so will have to cope with adversaries who are. Because of this basic axiom, Huntington's theory places prime emphasis on the creation of order, and the book is concerned with an examination of the actual ways in which order, or institutions, may be created. His analysis has two major branches—one involves the ways in which a leader may create institutions for an unruly society, the other involves the ways in which social struggle itself may lead to desirable institutional outcomes. When there is an existing leader, for instance a king, the decision to modernize the nation will not be the result of altruistic good will, but because he is afraid "that if he does not, someone else will" (Huntington, 1968, p. 155). Similarly, the leader creates a bureaucracy and a military not for purposes of rationalization and defense against foreign enemies but because the members of the bureaucracy and the military are, at least temporarily, "bought" allies of the king against other social forces.

POLITICAL PATHS TO POLITICAL DNELOPMENT

The problem is, for Huntington, that there are no development solutions. Once there are a bureaucracy and military, they may grow so strong as to threaten the leader himself; and if modernization begins to succeed in the society at large, it will create new groups such as the bourgeoisie, which are sworn enemies of kings or other unlimited rulers (Huntington, 1968, p. 167). Similarly the "reformer" faces the impossible dilemma that he must fight on two fronts, against conservatives who want to go backwards and radicals who want to go forward; and the "reformer" must be a master politician to manipulate the social forces and engage in deceptions that will maintain his or her control, such as overestimating the possibility of violent revolution in order to frighten landowners into an acceptance of land reform (Huntington, 1968, Chapter 6). And if he does achieve land reform, it may not have a progressive effect. All this is a long way from theories of effortless "take off" in the developing world.

Huntington's second approach to institutionalization involves the case where it occurs as the result of social group activity rather than that of a political leader. In this case of group-directed institutionalization, conflict occurs naturally between the "principal political forces," social classes, the church, the military, workers, and peasants. The outcome will depend on the alliances of the moment. Given three forces, say the government, the military, and labor, then if labor alone challenges the other two, it will lose; if labor is allied with the military it wins, although this is rare; or if labor and the government ally against the military, then only a very united military will survive. If every group is against every other group, then there is the praetorian struggle which destroys all social order (Huntington, 1968, p. 215). Every once in a while, the pattern of conflict results in some institutional development that suits all the opposing parties; should this continue there develops a civil polity. Without that kind of polity, according to Huntington, no economic progress can occur. He is unusual in drawing the causal line in the direction from politics to economics, where most developmentalists put economics first; and pays tribute to Lenin (and the authors of the Federalist Papers) for recognizing this point (Huntington, 1968, p. 338).

SOCIAL ORIGINS OF DICTATORSHIP AND DEMOCRACY

Another comparativist who was immensely influential upon the course of comparative politics in its early behavioral period was the historian Barrington Moore, whose massive analysis of the causes of democracy, fascism, and communism was a landmark in its day and remains a permanent classic of the discipline. *Social Origins of Dictatorship and Democracy: Lord and Peasant in the Making of the Modern World* (Moore, 1966) combined a rich use of history with a down-to-earth theory that was directly grounded in real historical events. The work's subtitle gives the flavor of Moore's theoretical direction by giving pre-eminence to sociological categories, "lord and peasant," in analysis; although the title left out a most important third player in the historical drama, the bourgeoisie.

Moore's general thesis was that large-scale political or governmental outcomes—democracy, fascism, or communism—could be predicted by studying the specific way socioeconomic forces interacted in a nation's history. His conclusions, which were much debated but are perhaps the least important element of the work, were that democracy was fostered by elimination of the peasantry, a balance between the crown and aristocracy, and a dynamic urban commercial sector; that fascism resulted from strong landed upper classes, exploitation of peasants, and the retention of feudal norms of aristocracy and obedience; and that communism followed from great agrarian bureaucracies that failed to make the transition to commercial agriculture, and which by escaping a bourgeois revolution were more vulnerable to peasant revolutions (Moore, 1966, p. 478).

However, the beauty of Moore's analysis was not in his conclusions, which were the subject of great debate and were indeed vulnerable to criticism; rather the beauty was in the details. Moore's comparisons were wide and rich, from France and Germany, to Eastern Europe, to India, China, and Japan. But unlike historians who may lose themselves in detail and miss any larger picture, Moore maintained a constant focus on socioeconomic classes and their interrelations across time. It was not necessarily a pretty picture—Moore remarks at one point that it seems a constant of human beings to unnecessarily torment one another—and his work stood in this sense against the prevailing development idea that modernization could occur benignly, without undue pain.[11]

THE DYNAMICS OF DEVELOPMENT

Moore begins his discussion of democracy with the observation that western feudalism contained elements that were favorable to democratic development, such as the existence of groups immune from the power of the ruler, the right of resistance to unjust authority, and political ties based upon freely undertaken contracts (Moore, 1966, p. 415). The goal, according to Moore, is a rough balance between the dominating monarch and a nobility with some necessary degree of independence. In many cases, of course, the established nobility precedes the strong monarchy, so that a balance of the two is greatly facilitated if members of the aristocracy engage in wars in which they decimate their own numbers, as in the English War of the Roses between the houses of Lancaster and York, where the death toll severely reduced the numbers of both factions. Of course, this is hardly a pattern favored by the United Nations or world public opinion in the present age; civil war is not in the developmentalist's rule book. But history is rife with civil catastrophe, and this enforced upon Moore and other historians a less sanguine view of the development process.

Assuming a rough balance between monarch and nobility (or leader and elites), Moore's next concern is economic, the relation of the nobility to the commercial elements of the society, located in the towns. If the nobility becomes too strong, and if it chooses to avoid commerce, then development halts; or, as Moore puts it succinctly, "no bourgeois, no democracy." The creation of a bourgeoisie is not an historical necessity for Moore, but the contingent result of specific actors and events; for instance, the demands of an absolutist ruler for taxes in hard coin, so that overlords needed cash rather than payments "in kind," such as grains or stock.

Among the "decisive" factors in development, according to Moore, is whether the landed aristocracy turns (or is forced to turn) to commercial agriculture; and if so, how they do it. In England the aristocracy threw peasants off much of the land, and itself turned to commercial farming; in France the elite squeezed produce from the peasants and sold it commercially; in Eastern Europe free peasants were reduced back to serf status so landowners could grow and export grain (Moore, 1966, pp. 418–420).

Moore argues that the English route proved most effective for democratic development, because commerce-minded landlords' interests were bound to the interests of the towns, and the aristocracy became independent of the crown and became intolerant (as the French were tolerant) of attempts at absolutist rule. Any failure to eliminate the peasants constitutes a problem for democratic development, Moore says, because peasants form a reservoir of support for dictatorship; although in some cases, such as Scandinavia and Switzerland, the peasants themselves turned to commerce.

Beyond the relationship of the landed aristocracy to monarchy, and the aristocracy's response to market commerce, Moore's third major factor in political development is the relationship between the landed upper classes and the towns; a relationship that is based on opposed interests, the town wanting cheap food and high prices for what it produces, the country wanting high prices for food and cheap manufactured goods. This cleavage is essential to democratic development, according to Moore, because should the upper classes unite, they would tend to act against the lower; but Moore also argues here for the importance of specific historical conditions—English conditions led the economy toward exports, for instance, while the French were drawn to provide armaments and luxury goods for the king (Moore, 1966, pp. 424–425).

CAUSAL PATHS TO POLITICAL OUTCOMES

The importance of commerce and the people who engage in it is that the bourgeoisie has a peculiarly important role to play in the whole process, a unique "stake in human freedom," according to Moore's analysis. It may of course be argued that by "human" freedom the bourgeoisie meant its own freedom only, but in the long run it hardly matters what was meant so long as the bourgeoisie was placed in explicit competition with the landed aristocracy, so that the bourgeoisie demanded changes, reforms, and modifications in the status quo that opened the political system to newer democratic factors. On the other hand (and here the mysterious English "genius" for mild government turns up), stability is favored by some degree of integration between bourgeoisie and aristocracy, as in England the aristocracy took up commerce and some of its norms, while the bourgeoisie acquired some of the aristocratic values of the older leadership groups and tolerated their presence in government circles. The price for this path included large amounts of "tolerable abuse" by the parties, which we would probably today call corruption; and much brutality imposed on the lower orders (Moore, 1966, pp. 424–427).

Working from this basic model it is possible to indicate briefly Moore's arguments on the origins of fascism and communism. The fascist cases are Japan and Germany, especially Prussia, where capitalism was in firm control, but conditions were unfriendly to the growth of free institutions. The crucial pattern was that the landed upper classes in both countries maintained absolute ascendancy over the peasants; in Japan by maintaining intact the traditional peasant society, in Eastern Europe by devising a form of plantation slavery. Such "labor repressive systems" are designed to squeeze as much as possible out of the underclass, and require strong political methods, sometimes disguised in traditional ideologies. But Moore emphasizes also that the effect of such arrangements was no more severe than that imposed on the lower orders by market logic, and that Japanese peasants suffered less than did the English ones (Moore, 1966, p. 435).

In Prussia the peasantry had virtually been freed in the fifteenth century, when as a result of grain exports peasants were again reduced to serfdom, and the towns were destroyed because the landlords did not use them for exports. The Hohenzollerns destroyed both nobility and towns, fused the royal bureaucracy and the aristocracy, supported aristocratic norms of ruling class superiority and the importance of status, in a military ethic that was inimical to democracy, according to Moore's account.

In Prussia, Japan, and also in Italy, the bureaucracy created an ethic of complete and unreflecting obedience, a discipline reflecting the "hard" qualities of the soldier. The bourgeoisie, too weak to rule alone, "threw itself into the arms of" the landed bourgeoisie, Moore says, so "that they exchanged the right to rule for the right to make money." But the bourgeoisie must be strong enough to be full partners in the fascist path; where the coalition fails altogether, as in Russia and China, Moore predicts another outcome—peasant revolution and communism (Moore, 1966, p. 437).

THE IMPORTANCE OF COALITION STRUCTURE

Where the coalition of aristocracy and bourgeoisie succeeds, Moore predicts a prolonged period of conservative rule, well short of fascism; where democratic features such as parliaments occur, these systems might evolve into unstable democracies, which themselves fail and end up in fascism because of landed elite retention of political power in the absence of any revolutionary breakthrough. Modernization "from above" without popular revolution may be very effective in ending feudal norms, rationalizing the political order, and creating modern, technically educated citizens. Moore argues that such regimes are particularly marked by the distinguished quality of their leaders, which is so frequent a phenomenon it cannot be mere coincidence, but results rather from the strength of aristocratic norms, even where the aristocrats dissent from the old order.

The turn to fascism, in Moore's explanation, occurs when the modernizing forces push the limits imposed by the never-discarded feudal regime and militarism is used to unite the upper classes, while the lower classes are compensated for their economic troubles by the romanticism of "land and freedom" into a kind of plebian anti-capitalism (Moore, 1966, pp. 441–442, 447–448). Communism occurs, finally in Moore's account, when the landed upper classes fail to make the transition to modern commerce and industry, and fail also to destroy the "prevailing social organization among the peasants." By "escaping" the bourgeois revolution, such countries are prey to peasant revolutions (Moore, 1966, pp. 467, 477–478).

Even this miserably brief summary of Moore's analysis shows why it held—and still holds—such fascination for social and political analysts of national political systems; but it shows also why the theory was so much criticized. Moore was writing theory that sought to cover a fairly large portion of human history, and claimed to have pretty precise explanations of what social forces, under what circumstances, come to what political results. The claim was to show not only how desirable results occurred, such as democracy, but how such virulent evils as fascism occurred, as well as communism, whatever one thought of it. This was unquestionably exhilarating. It was also open to attack from a thousand different directions, from critics claiming either that Moore's cases had not occurred quite as his interpretations claimed, or that even if his interpretations were correct for the countries covered by them, other countries showed entirely different patterns of development. Comparativists from the field of political science found other problems, especially the overgeneralizations about democracy, fascism, and communism rather failing to account theoretically for the differences between, for instance, Italian fascism and German naziism, or between the different democratic systems of England and France. But despite what anyone might say, the book was remarkably successful in providing nuanced interpretation of complex problems of political development.[12]

THE DEPENDENCY ARGUMENT

Parallel to mainstream North American diffusionist development theory ran a Latin American body of criticism that for the first time made the voice of the developing world heard by U.S. political scientists. Originating in a group of scholars associated with the United Nations Economic Commission for Latin America, dependency theory was less a scientifically oriented theory than it was a complaint at the injustice of the world economic and political system. Underdevelopment, these theorists argued, was not a "natural" condition but one that was created by the capitalist international system; and development theory was imperialism in a new form.

Their emphasis on the exploitation of the Third World seemed to be Marxist in origin, but was a gross distortion of Marx's actual writings, which were based on the grand hypothesis that capitalism, by exploiting peoples and classes, created wealth and ultimately freed mankind from the bondage of poverty and ignorance. The problem for those who sympathized with the poor was that Marx believed a long process had to be worked through before betterment would occur; history did not allow the skipping of stages.

Marx had faced the "dependency" issue directly in a discussion of the dreadful ravages made on traditional Indian village society by British colonial exploitation. His conclusions were in striking contrast to what most people expect a "Marxist" to hold. In the 1853 article titled "On Imperialism in India," Marx rhetorically sympathized with village India, where the social forms that had endured "from time immemorial," protecting the peasant from the agitations of the outside world, were now being torn asunder by "the brutal interference of the British tax-gatherer" and "the working of English steam and English free trade." This destruction of "industrious patriarchal and inoffensive social organizations" must be "sickening" to human feeling, continues Marx. Then he springs his startling conclusion:

> . . . we must not forget that these idyllic village communities, inoffensive though they may appear, had always been the solid foundation of Oriental despotism, that they restrained the human mind within the smallest possible compass, making it the unresisting tool of superstition, enslaving it beneath traditional rules, depriving it of all grandeur and historical energies. . . . We must not forget that these little communities were contaminated by distinc-

*tions of caste and by slavery, that they subjugated man to external circum-
stances instead of elevating man to be the sovereign of circumstances . . .*

*England, it is true, in causing a social revolution in Hindostan, was ac-
tuated only by the vilest interests, and was stupid in her manner of enforcing
them. But that is not the question. The question is, can mankind fulfill its
destiny without a fundamental revolution in the social state of Asia? If not,
whatever may have been the crimes of England she was the unconscious
tool of history in bringing about that revolution (Tucker, 1978, pp.
657–658).*

"Dependencistas" who call upon Marx's image to support their claim to be freed
from the injustices of history therefore pick a very hard-headed ally, one who in fact
offers them very little sympathy.

LATIN AMERICAN DEPENDENCY THEORISTS

Much of the dependency literature of the post–World War II period failed to achieve
such classical Marxian objectivity and could be classified as "vulgar" Marxism, a
term employed by Marxists themselves to denote those who seek to advance the interests of the working classes, often in defiance of the working classes themselves,
and who use as a major weapon some of the most impenetrable rhetorical jargon yet
invented in human history. This makes much dependency writing difficult for non-
Marxists to follow, and ensures that little intellectual cross-over occurs between the
left and the right. But there were exceptions to this pattern, among them Fernando
Henrique Cardoso and Enzo Faletto, the authors of *Dependency and Development in
Latin America* (1979), whose approach not only acknowledged the relevance of mainstream social science, but sought to extend the original Marxian approach to the situation in Latin America.

Cardoso and Faletto attempted to combine responsiveness to scholarly developmental approaches in other parts of the world with some of the sophistication of
analysis Marx himself had used in such works as the "18th Brumaire of Louis
Napoleon" or "The Civil War in France." The problem to which Cardoso and Faletto
directed their attention was not the lack of Latin American development but its halt;
after good economic progress during the early twentieth century and the economic
opportunities for underdeveloped nations created by the second world war, Latin
America seemed in the 1950s and 1960s to cease in its economic progress. It was
easy to blame the situation on the machinations of a world capitalist conspiracy determined to keep Latin America in its place in the international division of labor, but
Cardoso and Faletto did not do this. Rather, they emphasized the extent to which "external" forces had their primary effect not externally but as parts of the internal domestic political circumstances of each country. The authors also emphasized the
importance to the dependency process of the state and political alliances, "whether

the structural barriers to development remain or are overcome will be determined by how these economic conditions are used in the power game rather than by the particular economic conditions themselves" (Cardoso and Faletto, 1979, p. 175).

THE INTERNALIZATION OF DEPENDENCY

Cardoso and Faletto emphasize throughout the book that the theories of capitalist development in the industrialized world are virtually irrelevant to the Latin American situation, not only because of differences in historical period but because of structural differences between the two areas (Cardoso and Faletto, 1979, p. 172). They trace the history of selected Latin American states from the decline of direct colonial rule, when it was inextricably mixed with the wars and political struggles of Europe, through the independence movements, and the crises created by internal battles between economic, social, and regional elites in Latin America (Cardoso and Faletto, 1979, pp. 30–63).

By the end of the nineteenth century, European financial and commercial control of the region was replaced "by investment oriented toward control of production in the peripheral world that was considered important for the central economies." Where Latin American economies achieved integration into the world market, Cardoso and Faletto argue, economies differentiated alongside the export sector and new groups were created; but this occurred in different ways in different countries, strongly affected by which foreign economies predominated (Cardoso and Faletto, 1979, pp. 71, 74–75). The authors emphasize, however, that external dominance does not "mechanically" condition the internal sociopolitical situation, nor are events all due to sheer historical contingency.

> *There are structural limits to possible action, beginning with the available material base of production and the degree of development of the forces of production, and including the way in which these are combined with political and juridical relations within the country and its link with the hegemonic countries. Through the actions of groups, classes, organizations, and social movements in the dependent countries, these links are perpetuated, modified, or broken. Therefore, there is an internal dynamic that explains the course of events and thereby makes possible a political analysis (Cardoso and Faletto, 1979, pp. 173–174).*

This approach brought Cardoso and Faletto very close to the attitude of Marx himself, who in any number of works showed himself less a dogmatist than a scientist and a man led by intense historical curiosity, who spent a vast amount of effort studying history and contemporary events in the effort to discern what was happening in specific cases of political and economic change.[13] Capitalism was clearly showing itself in new forms in Latin America, and had taught observers to understand things they had not predicted. Cardoso has in fact said recently that dependency is not the barrier to development that had been thought (Carnoy, Castells, Cohen, and Cardoso, 1993). This, of course, had been vividly proven in a number of Asian nations (Onis, 1991).

But if the dependencistas were sometimes misguided, the dependency phase of development theory was fruitful: It made the practitioners of mainstream development theory more cautious about advancing their benign U.S.-centric view of political and economic change; it stimulated attention to the role of the state in social affairs; and it led to world systems theory, which systematically incorporated international events within domestic boundaries; and which was in addition strongly theoretical in its approach. The greater attention to the state will occupy a later chapter, but world systems theory must be included here, not for its character as a theory of international relations, where its validity is questionable, but as a theory relevant to the comparative politics of national development, national regression, and national stagnation.

THE MODERN WORLD SYSTEM

Immanuel Wallerstein's work on world systems proceeds on several levels, some of which are more important to the student of political development than others. At the "grandest" level, where the comparativist needs spend little time, Wallerstein is concerned to distinguish between two ways of organizing the world—empires and markets. In world empires, a single political system exists over most of the area in question; this was the predominant pattern for roughly 2000 years, according to Wallerstein. Because empires are politically centralized, they are strong, but this centralization is also the cause of their weakness, which results from the bureaucracy's absorbing too much of the profit taken from the income inflow from the periphery. In world economies, no such single political system exists (Wallerstein, 1974).

The advantage of world "economies," according to Wallerstein, is that within them, nation-states existed only to stabilize the market, and the market was the primary organizing force. This meant that the limit to the size of a world economy was largely set by communication, at the distance that could be traveled in forty to sixty days by contemporary means of transportation. Wallerstein divides world history into two periods, separated by the creation of the modern world economy in the late fifteenth and early sixteenth centuries. His subsequent analysis concerns the ways in which this world economy developed, using the well-known categories of center, periphery, and semi-periphery.

If Wallerstein's scope is grand, however, it is also microscopic and regional. Both levels are of interest to the comparativist, because while Wallerstein's focus is the historical development of Europe, his method of analysis is applicable to social research in any part of the world, in any time period. Its most notable characteristic is the specificity of the discussion. Similar to Braudel and other members of the *Annales* school of French historical analysis, Wallerstein is out in the countryside with the peasants, or out on the water with the fishermen. Review of the arguments in his *The*

Modern World System I: Capitalist Agriculture and the Origins of the European World-Economy in the Sixteenth Century (Wallerstein, 1974) shows how he proceeds.

Capitalism does not emerge in some mysteriously inevitable way from feudalism, in Wallerstein's view; rather he emphasizes the specific, almost idiosyncratic, processes by which it grows. It is even inaccurate to say that capitalism emerges from a "dual" economy (markets in the towns, subsistence in the rural areas), he wants to go back further, to why markets exist. In Wallerstein's picture, peasants worked in both modes. They farmed for themselves first, and if things went well they had surplus to sell. In addition, when landlords took their portion of the crop, it would under certain conditions be more than they could use, and they would sell it. Since aristocrats do not willingly lower themselves to engage in haggling, they used agents, and these agents often became independent merchants, as did prosperous peasants. This served to create towns, but because roads were bad, commerce could only be local or in easy-to-transport luxury goods, as long as feudal conditions existed. Wallerstein also includes in his analysis considerations of climate and physical health (the presence or absence of such factors as the plague), which influence not only production but the ownership of land, since severe epidemics reduce the population and enable the survivors to increase their holdings (Wallerstein, 1974, pp. 15–19).

OCEAN CURRENTS AND WARS

The establishment of a world economy in the fifteenth and sixteenth centuries was based on three factors, according to Wallerstein's argument: the predominant cause was the expansion of the geographical size of the European world; related to this was the development of a division of labor between areas; third was the creation of relatively strong state machineries in the "core" area (Wallerstein, 1974, p. 38). Wallerstein then shifts to the regional level of analysis, in seeking to show that the European response to the economic crises of the fourteenth century was not "European"—it was Portuguese. It was not some amorphous force that solved the problem of expansion, in other words, it was specific peoples in specific circumstances.

In Portugal, he argues, the lords had fewer sources of additional land than in other areas of Europe, there was class conflict, and since Portugal was sited on favorable ocean currents, expansion was a natural result. In this structural approach, no events are inevitable, there is no reified force of "progress," but just things that sometimes happen if circumstances are right. In China, Wallerstein suggests, there was a traditional attitude that it was already the "whole world," and this arrogance, combined with an abundance of land that made further exploration unnecessary, prevented the emergence of capitalism (Wallerstein, 1974, pp. 38–57).

"Core" states are created by these varying conditions.

> *Thus if, at a given moment in time, because of a series of factors at a previous time, one region has a slight edge over another in terms of one key fac-*

tor, and there is a conjuncture of events which make this slight edge of cen-
tral importance in terms of determining social action, then the slight edge is
converted into a large disparity and the advantage holds even after the con-
juncture has passed (Wallerstein, 1974, p. 98).

In other words, from this analytic viewpoint, countries do not become cores because
they set out to do so, or enter some conspiracy against the periphery; they become
core states because of some action they take in response to environmental and social
needs, and these actions *sometimes* have the effect of putting them at the center of
their world, for a time. The time need not be long. Portugal failed, according to
Wallerstein's analysis, because it was content with the markets it had along the
African coast and did not pursue its advantage. Spain similarly lost its precedence in
the world economy by wasting resources in its conflicts with the French (Wallerstein,
1974, pp. 169–172).

THE "REEFS" OF STRUCTURE

In this sort of analysis Wallerstein provides an excellent example of structural analysis of a classic kind (quite unrelated to the misnamed structural-functional theory discussed earlier). Structuralism focuses on what Wallerstein calls the "coral reefs of
human relations," the hidden or unnoticed factors that influence the shape of social
and political systems. Structures are not permanent but change very slowly when they
do change, and many times they are left out of the analysis because we are so accus-
tomed to them we do not realize their impact.

Structures are both physical and socioeconomic. Wallerstein discusses, for instance, the decline of the city states of northern Italy, especially Venice and Genoa,
which from being the core declined into semi-peripheral states because, in part, the
weather changed and the rain created swamps that created malaria and a high death
rate; but also in part because they lost their markets in England and France as these
countries' own markets developed, and the northern Italians could no longer com-
pete against cheaper goods from abroad (Wallerstein, 1974, pp. 214–220). Montesquieu included such factors in his political theory, and was often mocked for so
doing, but structuralism endorses the idea that matters like climate cannot be left
out of account.

World system theory is rather too broad to be of use to students of comparative
politics, but the methodological approach used by Wallerstein is educational in several ways. It is interesting that the exercise began in Africa, where Wallerstein's attempts to understand the relationships between the conceptual frameworks of the
Europeans and the Africans were the origin of his shift to a systemic level of analysis.
The colonial process as he described it forms an example of political interaction in
many different circumstances: Certain people hold power and utilize ideological as
well as physical mechanisms to make that power seem legitimate; other groups seek

to challenge that authority; structural conjunctures favor one or the other group; the various participants respond differentially to the structural opportunities; and one side or the other wins a sequence of interactions (Wallerstein, 1974, p. 5). The process led to the end of colonialism; it leads sometimes to development, and sometimes not, thereafter.

Wallerstein's importance for comparative politics is his devotion to collecting all the layers of relevant data, from the climate to social organizations to the state, and not neglecting the position of the individual political system in larger international contexts. This is difficult to achieve in history because of the unsettled questions about what "actually" happened several hundred years ago. It should be easier in the contemporaneous research that characterizes comparative politics.

THE CHALLENGE

Development theory has been a major force in the study of comparative politics, and continues to be so because the problems of national poverty, disease, and civil conflict are so acute. Facing these problems, the prime motive of many students of comparative politics is to "want to help." This is an honest and civilized wish, but the history of development theory has shown that the desire to help is, alone, insufficient to be able to do so. Development theory, from its inception to the present, has taught its students more than they really wanted to know about the nature of whole human societies, their complexity, their difficulties, and their resistance to change. Comparative politics has discovered especially that a society, even if poor, is not a tabula rasa on which the modernized world can write its own prescription. Such societies are only apparently simple; in fact each is bound by complex and often rigid networks of interlocking relationships that dictate the subsistence of its members and provide the structure of their lives.

The theorists of development discussed in the present chapter played a major role in this discovery of the world's complexity. From the early days, when peasants were assumed ready and eager to fall into the arms of the modern free marketplace, to the later disillusioned days when the international market came to seem not the solution but the problem, development theory helped its proponents and their critics to probe many of their unexamined assumptions.

The stereotypes of Adam Smith and Karl Marx both failed, leaving comparative politics with the daunting task of finding adequate substitutes for theoretic guidance. The most useful studies seemed to be those that threw theory aside and concentrated on practical problems—Huntington with the political strategies of leaders facing rebels, revolutionaries, and other inconvenient citizens; Moore with the socioeconomic problems of lord, peasant, and bourgeois; Wallerstein with one eye on ocean currents and climate and the other on socioeconomic structural conditions. This emphasis on the nuts and bolts of politics would come to play an increasing part in further developments in the comparative field.

NOTES

1. The development literature is voluminous and diverse. Good current discussions include Chilcote (1994, pp. 217–230), and Almond's retrospective analysis (1987, pp. 437–490). Early viewpoints are discussed in Bill and Hardgrave (1973, pp. 43–83). The field has always suffered from the fact, early noted by Pye, that there are at least ten different definitions of what development means, quite apart from the many related concepts such as modernization (Pye, 1966, pp. 31–48).

2. Use of the term "developing" rather than underdeveloped or undeveloped appears to be attributable to Almond, at least in respect to the political science discipline (see his interview in Baer, Jewell and Sigelman 1991).

3. Parsons' definition of structural-functionalism is the center of his influential work, *The Social System* (1951). It entails analysis of social systems as social wholes and is distinguished from individual motivational, or dynamic, analysis (see pp. 19–22 on the former, pp. 202–203 on the latter). Dynamic analysis is the focus of Parsons and Shils (1951).

4. Functional forms of analysis are not easy to untangle, because of the wide variety of definitions employed, both operationally and metaphysically; and also because the functional label is avoided by some theorists who use the method, such as Easton (1965a, b). An early discussion of functionalism as linked to systems theory is found in Bill and Hardgrave (1973, pp. 201–228). Brief but enthusiastic mention is made in Dogan and Pelassy (1984, pp. 37–43). Still the most analytic discussion is Merton (1957, pp. 46–55 and passim).

5. In the initial chapter of the book, Almond presented two parallel sets of terms, explaining the origin of the functional concepts: what used to be called the state was now the political system, what used to be called powers (as in the "separation of powers") were now functions, what used to be called offices were now roles, what used to be institutions were now called structures, and what used to be called public opinion and citizenship training was now called political culture and socialization (Almond and Coleman, 1960, p. 4). This would not be entirely accurate, since some thinkers defined the new concepts in new ways; but it does illustrate vividly how old wine gets into new bottles.

6. The series included: Pye (1963), LaPalombara (1963), Ward and Rustow (1964), Coleman (1965), Pye and Verba (1965), LaPalombara and Weiner (1966), Binder (1971), Tilly (1975), and Grew (1978). The last two of these were edited by historians, and marked the transition to the new interest in the state.

7. The authors' earlier works were among the classics of the field, for instance Binder (1961, 1962), Coleman (1958), Pye (1962), and Weiner (1962).

8. In addition to Verba (1971), see Tilly (1975) and Grew (1978).

9. I have suggested (Lane, 1994) that the structural functional approach can be made concrete by inverting its perspective to a micro-analytic level, and using the strategic analyses suggested by the several contributors to the Binder volume.

10. Holt and Turner scored several points in their argument by the rather unfair tactic of comparing structural-functional theory to the theory of Kenneth Arrow, an economic theory of extreme sophistication. Very few theories could survive such a test. The issue of evaluating theory is taken up in Chapter 6.

11. "Though I cannot prove it, I suspect that one of the few lasting and dependable sources of human satisfaction is making other people suffer . . ." (Moore, 1966, p. 338). The context of the remark is the Indian caste system and other forms of social distinction among persons.

12. It also inspired generations of younger scholars, such as Skocpol (1979, p. xv), and Scott (Moore, 1966, 1993 Edition, p. ix).

13. See Marx's extensive writings for the popular press, especially the *New York Herald Tribune*. Many are collected in Tucker (1972).

REFERENCES

Aberle, D. F., A. K. Cohen, A. K. Davis, M. J. Levy, Jr., and F. S. Sutton. "The Functional Prerequisites of a Society." *Ethics* 60 (1950): 100–111.

Almond, Gabriel A. "The Development of Development." In Myron Weiner and Samuel Huntington (Eds.). *Understanding Political Development* (pp. 437–490). Glenview: Little Brown, 1987.

Almond, Gabriel A., and James S. Coleman (Eds.). *The Politics of the Developing Areas.* Princeton: Princeton University Press, 1960.

Almond, Gabriel A., and G. Bingham Powell, Jr. *Comparative Politics: A Developmental Approach.* Boston: Little Brown, 1966.

Almond, Gabriel A., and G. Bingham Powell, Jr. *Comparative Politics Today: A World View.* Boston: Little Brown, 1980 (3rd Edition, 1984).

Baer, Michael A., Malcolm E. Jewell, and Lee Sigelman (Eds.) *Political Science in America: Oral Histories of a Discipline.* Lexington: University Press of Kentucky, 1991.

Bill, James A., and Robert L. Hardgrave, Jr. *Comparative Politics: The Quest for Theory.* Columbus: Charles E. Merrill, 1973.

Binder, Leonard. *Religion and Politics in Pakistan.* Berkeley: University of California Press, 1961.

Binder, Leonard. *Iran: Political Development in a Changing Society.* Berkeley: University of California Press, 1962.

Binder, Leonard, et al. *Crisis and Sequences in Political Development.* Princeton: Princeton University Press, 1971.

Cardoso, Fernando Henrique, and Enzo Faletto. *Dependency and Development in Latin America.* Berkeley: University of California Press, 1979. (Originally published 1971 as *Dependencia y desarrollo en America Latina*).

Bendix, Reinhard. *Max Weber: An Intellectual Portrait.* New York: Doubleday Anchor, 1960.

Carnoy, Martin, Manuel Castells, Stephen S. Cohen, and Fernando Henrique Cardoso. *The New Global Economy in the Information: Reflections of Our Changing World.* University Park: Pennsylvania State University Press, 1993.

Chilcote, Ronald H. *Theories of Comparative Politics: The Search for a Paradigm Reconsidered* (2nd Edition). Boulder: Westview Press, 1994.

Coleman, James S. *Nigeria: Background to Nationalism.* Berkeley: University of California Press, 1958.

Coleman, James Smoot (Ed.). *Education and Political Development.* Princeton: Princeton University Press, 1965.

Coleman, James S. "The Development Syndrome: Differentiation-Equality-Capacity." In Leonard Binder et al., *Crisis and Sequence in Political Development* (pp. 73–100). Princeton: Princeton University Press, 1971.

Dogan, Mattei, and Dominique Pelassy. *How to Compare Nations: Strategies in Comparative Politics*. Chatham: Chatham House, 1984.

Easton, David. *A Framework for Political Analysis*. Englewood Cliffs: Prentice Hall, 1965a.

Easton, David. *A Systems Analysis of Political Life*. New York: John Wiley and Sons, 1965b.

Grew, Raymond (Ed.). *Crises of Political Development in Europe and the United States*. Princeton: Princeton University Press, 1978.

Holt, Robert T., and John E. Turner. "Crises and Sequences in Collective Theory Development." *American Political Science Review* 69 (September 1975): 979–95.

Huntington, Samuel P. *Political Order in Changing Societies*. New Haven: Yale University Press, 1968.

Huntington, Samuel P. *The Third Wave: Democratization in the Late Twentieth Century*. Norman: The University of Oklahoma Press, 1991.

Lane, Ruth. "Structural-Functionalism Reconsidered: A Proposed Research Model." *Comparative Politics* 26, no. 4 (July 1994): 461–67.

LaPalombara, Joseph (Ed.). *Bureaucracy and Political Development*. Princeton: Princeton University Press, 1963.

LaPalombara, Joseph, and Myron Weiner (Eds.). *Political Parties and Political Development*. Princeton: Princeton University Press, 1966.

LaPalombara, Joseph. "Penetration: A Crisis of Governmental Capacity," and "Distribution: A Crisis of Resource Management." In Leonard Binder et al. *Crisis and Sequences in Political Development* (pp. 205–82). Princeton: Princeton University Press, 1971.

Lerner, Daniel. *The Passing of Traditional Society: Modernizing the Middle East*. New York: Free Press, 1958.

Marx, Karl. See Tucker (1978).

Merton, Robert K. *Social Theory and Social Structure* (Revised and Enlarged Edition 1957). New York: The Free Press, 1949.

Moore, Barrington, Jr. *The Social Origins of Dictatorship and Democracy*. Boston: Beacon Press, 1966.

Onis, Ziya. "The Logic of the Developmental State (Review Article)." *Comparative Politics* 24, no. 1 (October 1991): 109–26.

Parsons, Talcott. *The Social System*. New York: 26. The Free Press of Glencoe, 1951.

Parsons, Talcott, and Edward Shils (Eds.). *Toward a General Theory of Action*. New York: Harper Torchbooks, 1962, (1951).

Pye, Lucien W. *Politics, Personality, and Nation Building: Burma's Search For Identity*. New Haven: Yale University Press, 1962.

Pye, Lucien W. (Ed.). *Communications and Political Development*. Princeton: Princeton University Press, 1963.

Pye, Lucien W. *Aspects of Political Development*. Boston: Little Brown, 1966.

Pye, Lucien W. "Identity and the Political Culture," and "The Legitimacy Crisis." In Leonard Binder et al. *Crisis and Sequences in Political Development* (pp. 101–58). Princeton: Princeton University Press, 1971.

Pye, Lucien W., and Sidney Verba (Eds.). *Political Culture and Political Development*. Princeton: Princeton University Press, 1965.

Rostow, Walt W. *The Stages of Economic Growth*. New York: Cambridge University Press, 1960.

Skocpol, Theda. *States and Social Revolutions*. Cambridge: Cambridge University Press, 1979.

Tilly, Charles (Ed.). *Formation of National States in Western Europe*. Princeton: Princeton University Press, 1975.

Tucker, Robert C. (Ed.). *The Marx-Engels Reader* (Second Edition). New York: Norton, 1978.

Verba, Sidney. "Sequences and Development." In Leonard Binder et al. *Crisis and Sequences in Political Development* (pp. 283–316). Princeton: Princeton University Press, 1971.

Wallerstein, Immanuel. *The Modern World System I: Capitalist Agriculture and the Origins of the European World Economy in the 16th Century*. New York: Academic Press, 1979.

Ward, Robert E., and Dankwart A. Rustow (Eds.). *Political Modernization in Japan and Turkey*. Princeton: Princeton University Press, 1964.

Weiner, Myron. *The Politics of Scarcity: Public Pressure and Political Response in India*. Chicago: University of Chicago Press, 1962.

Weiner, Myron. "Political Participation: Crisis of the Political Process." In Leonard Binder et al. *Crisis and Sequences in Political Development* (pp. 159–204). Princeton: Princeton University Press, 1971.

▶ 4

Comparative Politics Reconsiders the State

In studying any subject matter from physics to biology to politics, the choice of a theoretical framework or conceptual structure is of primary importance because it defines what the analyst looks for, what is ignored, what connections are plausible, what truths are valid. Among the primary characteristics distinguishing scientists from laypersons is the scientists' greater consciousness of such intellectual structures as an element in their thinking. Untrained people tend to assume thinking is a "natural" process and that there is only one way to do it—usually their own way. Coming to understand that thinking proceeds in a considerable variety of perhaps equally acceptable ways is the beginning of science because it requires thoughtful attention to what data is collected, how it is connected, and how it is interpreted (Churchland, 1979; Giere, 1988; Hilton, 1988).[1]

Comparative politics has proceeded for much of its history along "natural" lines. It studied the countries it thought important, and used a homegrown natural conceptual structure, the idea that one or two idealized forms of government were the goals toward which all nations of the world would or should naturally proceed. Behavioralism was an initial rebellion against such "natural" approaches, but the attempt to escape the everyday political biases proved difficult because of the scarcity of good ideas, frameworks, concepts, or theories to replace them. The development literature contrived to slip around this barrier by using theories in which the "natural" ideas were stated in such abstract form that they seemed both impressive and plausible, at least for an initial period of time. Along with this approach, some comparativists turned to great ideas from the past, especially Marxism's grand theory, to supplement their thinking about the contemporary political world and its problems.

The major focus at this stage of the discipline's progress was "the state," which proved to be a difficult experience for comparative politics; the phase was reluctant, brief, and brought about its own dissolution. Traditionally, the state has been seen as a unified single actor, an actor that effectively controls the territory under its jurisdiction. This was the meaning of the notion of "sovereignty" upon which many theories of international politics were constructed, and which was central to European theories of government. The essential mark of a sovereign state was that it had the "last say" in any national dispute; other actors might be allowed to argue and negotiate but only for a finite amount of time. At some point the state would step in and the state's decision would "settle" the matter (Brierly, 1963).

In the sharpest contrast with such theories of state unity and potency is the American view of national government. This view was neatly expressed in a remark by former Secretary of State George Shulz, who was asked at a news conference if a particularly lively recent issue had finally been settled. No, it had not been settled, Shulz said; "nothing is ever settled around here."

The American conception of government shines through this response. People who wish to quarrel with a government decision may take it to Congress, to local or state officials, to courts, and finally to the Supreme Court; and if that august body goes against them, the discontented can go back to Congress or the state or wherever, to begin the cycle of civil protest over again at the beginning. This political round dance characterizes the U.S. political system and constitutes a constantly repeated denial of "sovereignty" in the European sense.

Such a background in governmental fluidity left American political scientists quite underprepared to confront a comparative politics theory based on the unified state. The only time when Americans ever seemed to feel that the state was unified was when it was trying to put something over on the public, when it was trying to wage an unpopular war, or save itself from impeachment. Such cases did not prove a good ground for theory about the state to build upon. However, the study of the state did provide an exemplary case of what happens when theory and experience find themselves in conflict; and what happens is that theory must give way to experiential preconceptions.

In respect to the study of "the state" in comparative politics, at least, the theory was modified to fit observed practice and the state rapidly dissolved into its component parts, the various subgroups that work within legislatures, bureaucracies, White House basements, statehouses, and all other political offices—and all of which may work in contrary directions.

The attempt to discover whether the state could become the central theoretic focus of the discipline was important in the development of comparative politics, however, because comparativists of all stripes became increasingly aware of the vital role played in science by theoretical-conceptual frameworks, and by this concern began to push themselves even further toward the foundations of a solid science of comparative politics. A major step in this awareness was the discovery that mainstream development theory and structural-functionalism generally had left something out of their perspectives, and now that people began to think about the matter, it seemed odd that it could have been left out at all. And so emerged the movement known as "bringing the state back in."

It must be emphasized, of course, that the state had never really been thrown out. Huntington had emphasized state and political perspectives on development (1968), and Lijphart (1977) had directed attention to forms of the state, such as consociational democracy, which modified common democratic practices in order to accommodate ethnic and religious differences. But in general, the "stylish" theories had taken another direction, toward wholesale emphasis on "society" and a belief that government actions reflected social demands in a transparent way, and that governments had no motives of their own.

THE RETURN TO THE STATE

The book that bore the ringing title, *Bringing the State Back In*, was edited by Peter Evans, Dietrich Rueschemeyer, and Theda Skocpol and published in 1985. It was sponsored by the institution that had earlier been important in the behavioral and structural-functional literature, the Social Science Research Council;[2] and had its origins in a 1982 conference where the autonomous importance of the state was first emphasized. No longer, said the book's preface, was it appropriate to see the state merely as the reflection of social forces—or, as they might have said, as Easton's blank black box—it was time to study how states were formed and reorganized, and how states affected societies through their interventions and through relations with social groups. The influence between states and societies was presumed to run in both directions: States were potentially autonomous in relation to their societies, but were "influenced and limited" in their structure and activities by socioeconomic relations (Evans et al., 1985, pp. vi, viii).

Bringing the State Back In contained a number of chapters by other authors, one of which will be discussed in detail below, but in assessing the state-centered movement it is helpful to begin with the conceptual chapter co-written by the three editors (Evans et al., 1985, pp. 346–366). While the chapter raises more questions than it provides answers, experience would show that at least in the long run, questions may be more useful than answers. The basic difficulty, however, was that the discipline returned to the state without having anything resembling a theory of the state.[3]

Evans, Rueschemeyer, and Skocpol begin with a statement of the method to be used, that of "analytical induction," drawing upon existing theoretical debates especially among neo-Marxists and neo-Weberians, and "doing comparative and historical studies to address theoretically relevant questions" (Evans et al., 1985, pp. 347, vi). Analytical induction, the authors explain, is "highly theoretically engaged," although it inverts the approach of "grand theorizing"—a comment readily interpretable as distinguishing the statist approach from ghosts of the past such as structural-functionalism or other forms of grand theory. The authors also seek to emphasize that their approach does not involve mere historical case studies, which were traditionally thought to be the exact opposite of grand theory, but uses instead historical cases only as a means for tracing deep processes and structures, since without historical depth the scholar would be restricted to static analysis of states at one point in time, rather than capturing their crises and changes (Evans et al., 1985, p. 347).[4]

The concern with depth and history in studying the state was in massive contradiction with the earlier behavioralist studies, which emphasized empiricism and the search for universal theory. It is not always clear in the early behavioralism that empiricism is inherently superficial. Empiricism in political science did not so much emphasize facts as it did observable facts. If a thing could be measured, then it was acceptable as a scientific fact but not otherwise. Such a rule was beneficial in teaching people not to use fuzzy rhetorical terms, but it forced political scientists to restrict themselves to isolated, easily measurable variables rather than studying the context and underlying structures that influenced surface politics. The state theorists sought to escape this restriction.

It is one thing to argue that a deeper study of the state is needed, however, and quite another to know in what terms or concepts the state is to be studied. The new state theorists, in this plight, adopted the most banal of the questions raised by Marxists and neo-Marxists in relation to the state, the issue of whether the state was merely the "executive committee" of the capitalist class, doing its will, or whether the state had some degree of independence from forces in the surrounding society. One of the dreariest aspects of the question, as a tool of scientific inquiry, was that it was freighted with more or less unstated normative concerns—the belief that "the state" was a "progressive" force dragging everyone toward a more rational civilized future. Hegel, who believed the state was more important than any of its citizens, and that the state's "freedom" was the meaning of all world history, stands in the dim background of most discussions of the state, either explicitly or implicitly.[5]

On the other hand, American political scientists have no real experience with "the" state: their national government is only national government, and the states are those provincial entities that pick up what powers they can, where the national government is uninterested. So it was natural and perhaps creative that, in default of American theory, the neo-statists adopted European myths to fill the void.

THE SEARCH FOR USABLE THEORY

The editors of *Bringing the State Back In* start with the neo-Marxist debate on state autonomy, which sets those who argue that states are only instruments of dominant class interests against two opponents: those who see states as embodying class relations and being reshaped continually by political class struggles, and those who see the state as organizationally autonomous from dominant classes yet still committed to aid capitalist accumulation so as to preserve class dominance in mode of production overall (see the review in Chilcote, 1994, pp. 284–336).

Turning from neo-Marxists to neo-Weberians in the search for new ideas raises a second issue, that of state "capacity," strong states or weak states, as an alternative to taking state autonomy as an axiom. Where states are "strong," administrators have the ability to pursue policies at variance with the interests of the dominant socioeconomic classes (Evans et al., 1985, p. 350).[6]

The meaning of state strength is made confusing by differences among Marxists and Weberians, the editors remark, since Marxists mean by a strong state one that well serves the capitalist class (making the United States state very strong, for instance), while Weberians measure strength against an "ideal type" of a "centralized and fully rationalized Western Bureaucracy" such as eighteenth-century Prussia, able to "work its will efficiently and without effective social opposition" (here the United States would not be considered strong). In contrast to these approaches, Evans, Rueschemeyer, and Skocpol define their research tactic as studying those in charge of state structures, and the conditions under which those in charge attempt to pursue their own goals; focusing on the specific organizational structures that undergird the state's capacity.

The editors argue that the various chapters in the volume provide theoretical hypotheses in respect to actual state behavior: that there is a mixed relation between different state capacities, and some states might be strong in one area such as agriculture, but not elsewhere; in other cases state intervention in a particular area stimulates social forces to fight back and frustrate further state expansion; or states may strengthen their repressive activities while withdrawing from economic intervention. The "strength of capacity" of a state, they conclude, is not a workable analytic variable; although since basic fiscal and administrative capacities can be used in many tasks, neither is it altogether irrelevant (Evans et al., 1985, pp. 352–353).

A further dimension of research on state organizations involves the relationship of states to their socioeconomic environments, to dominant and subordinate classes, and to politically active or potentially mobilized groups. The editors reject the "received theoretical frameworks" and their standard solutions to this question: Marxists arguing state officials grow in strength by working for the dominant class; "crude" Weberians arguing the strong state reduces all outside groups to subordination. Instead, the essays show a dialectical relationship between autonomy and capacity, where the power of the state and the power of social groups may be positively related, both rising together or declining together. Where the state is fragmented, for instance, this might cause the labor movement to be fragmented as well. Evans, Rueschemeyer, and Skocpol also argue that state strength (intervention) may lead to its own diminution because intervention mobilizes social groups, as in Brazil and Austria, discussed in studies included in the volume, where social groups are brought so fully into the state that the state's strength is reduced (Evans et al., 1985, p. 354).

But in concluding that the "received" state theories were either not much help in guiding research or were actively misleading, the editors admit they are left without any new theory to offer, or even a complete set of hypotheses. There are only "heuristic" principles: that states may be autonomous (and are therefore worth "bringing back in"); that the relation between states and societies needs to be studied in specific historical cases; that both formal and informal structures composing the state need to be studied; that particular attention should be paid to states under challenge; and that conceptual categories need to be provided for the study of state capacity and state-society relations (Evans et al., 1985, pp. 356–362).

If, as this list suggests, there was very little theory available to guide empirical research, nonetheless the empirical research was itself rich, as shown by several of the contributors to the Evans, Rueschemeyer, and Skocpol volume, for instance, Peter Evans's "Foreign Capital and the Third World State," which was revised and reprinted in a later collection of essays on research frontiers in comparative politics (Weiner and Huntington, 1987, pp. 319–352). Thus, the very volume that brought the state back in contained types of analysis that brought back not so much the state, but politics; a politics that tended to shatter the hope of building a theory of comparative politics on the unified state.

THE EFFECT OF FOREIGN CAPITAL IN THE DEVELOPING WORLD

Evans' analysis of the relationship between outside capital and underdeveloped states amply illustrates the behavioralists' basic axiom that it is better by far to go out and investigate a matter rather than to argue about it endlessly. His topic is the politically charged issue of the interference by transnational corporations in the economies and social lives of Third World nations, and the related question of whether foreign capital undercuts the sovereignty of these states, as the dependencistas claimed.

Evans combines in the article a variety of studies, all influenced by the dependency movement (although he remarks that some disagreed violently with it), and labels the perspective the "new political economy" approach because it combines a classical political economy approach along with the dependency school's sensitivity to international factors and the state as an actor.[7] The argument directly opposes the dependencista thesis that foreign capital cripples the state. Evans looks at specific relations in three areas: (1) extractive industries, (2) manufacturing, (3) and loan capital. In each case his results are contrary to what might have been expected according to existing theoretical approaches.

The standard view of transnational corporation penetration of Third World nations in respect to extractive industries involved a foreign-owned enclave using local workers only as unskilled labor, exploiting mineral resources and exporting all the output, along with the passive acquiescence of a comprador state apparatus that received only token tax revenues and a sliver of the corporate profits.

This has been replaced, Evans argues, by a new view of foreign-owned extractive sectors increasingly providing sites for expansion of nationalist and homegrown entrepreneurial activities (Evans, 1987, pp. 322–323). This growth in domestic political activity results from the need for the state, however weak, to monitor international companies; this produces a larger state apparatus and bureaucracy, and monitoring agencies increasingly train managers who eventually enable the state itself to operate the industries. As the state share of the revenue grows, the state has more money to spend on its own policies and purposes, sometimes resulting in state economies such as Algeria's, where "the state makes over 90 percent of the country's industrial investments" (Evans, 1987, p. 324).

Evans further discusses theories of the "obsolescing bargain" in which a state, initially too poor to exploit its own natural resources, gets richer through transnational corporate development of the resource and is able in turn to, as it were, blackmail the corporation that has sunk money into investments that are vulnerable to state actions. A "learning curve" works thus in favor of the state, using not only its own experience to outmaneuver the foreign corporations but also the experience of other Third World nations who have learned to exploit their exploiters. This, Evans notes, works best only in extractive industries where the investors cannot easily pick up and leave if conditions are not just to their liking, because their assets are sunk in oil wells and excavated mines (Evans, 1987, p. 325).

THE INTERPLAY OF POLITICAL-ECONOMIC FORCES

Foreign investment has another beauty for Third World nations, according to Evans. When the state becomes sufficiently aggressive to consider nationalization of industries, the "foreignness" of foreign-owned firms gives the state an ideological excuse to do so (nationalism, sovereignty, the right to be masters in their own homes). In addition, when the industries are owned by outsiders, nationalization will provoke no local groups to oppose it—as it certainly would if the industries were owned by indigenous capitalists. There is, of course, the danger that too much activity on the part of Third World states will drive transnational corporations to find quieter areas for doing business, and if this happens the firms will likely set up new industries whose production competes with that of their initial investment area. So the strengths and weaknesses are not always on the same sides, the game is not zero-sum, and both sides may profit from cooperation, Evans concludes (Evans, 1987, pp. 331–332).

In the two other economic areas that Evans reviews—manufacturing and foreign loan capital—the Third World state's bargaining position is less strong than it is against extractive industries because the corporations' investments are less sunk in specific extracting facilities and can be withdrawn more easily. Nonetheless, there may still be local benefits. Manufacturing sector relations, for instance, are slanted initially against the state: The foreign corporations get a larger proportion of revenues; because of technology innovation, bargains do not obsolesce; and the learning curve does not apply. However, local elites over time may acquire the expertise to outmaneuver the transnational corporations, the state may become more unified, and on occasions the state may coopt the foreign corporation to act counter to the interest of its own home base, as Mexico did against Detroit (Evans, 1987, p. 335). Even in response to foreign loan capital, which has the greatest fluidity of the three areas and gives creditors considerable leverage over the state, Evans finds that it causes the state to grow because international loans go to the state as the safest borrower, and this gives the state resources to use against such enemies as traditional or ethnic elites (Evans, 1987, pp. 342–343).

This early work on "bringing the state back in" thus had paradoxical lessons to teach comparative politics. On one hand, there was to be greater attention to the state as an institutional whole, but on the other hand, research into the state tended to dissolve the institution into separate and not necessarily coordinated parts. The inconsistency, which drew comparativists irresistibly away from the initial conceptual position that the state had an important unity, would continue in another major contribution to the statist literature.

REVOLUTIONS AND THE STUDY OF THE STATE

One of the best-known and most-often-cited works in the new state tradition was Skocpol's *States and Social Revolutions: A Comparative Analysis of France, Russia, and China* (1979), a study of how the modernizing process had occurred in these cases through "rapid, basic transformations of a society's state and class structures" (p. 3). Trained as a historian and macro-sociologist, Skocpol takes an approach designed to improve upon previous theories of revolution, which she defines as including, variously, Marxist theories, psychological theories, systems-oriented theories, and political conflict theories.[8] She adopts a "nonvoluntarist, structural" perspective along with a view of states as contained by, but potentially autonomous from, socioeconomic interests and structures; she thus "revises" Marxism to include political conflict (Skocpol, 1979, pp. 14–33). Skocpol employs the "comparative historical" method, with its interest in political and institutional factors, seeking explanations "that illuminate truly general patterns of causes and outcomes" without "abstracting away" the particular aspects of each historical event; but adds a special concern for "analysis" where the purpose "is to develop, test, and refine causal, explanatory hypotheses about events or structures integral to macro-units such as nation-states" (Skocpol, 1979, p. 36).

The revolutions in France in 1789, in Russia in 1917, and China in 1911 are defined as "successful revolutions" and are used as positive cases, in order to discover the relevant common causal factors of revolutions in these three "wealthy and politically ambitious agrarian states." Skocpol's basic model involves the conjuncture of (1) administrative-military incapacity of the old regime states, (2) widespread peasant rebellion, and (3) a political leadership attempting to consolidate power; resulting in (4) "centralized, bureaucratic, and mass incorporating" new state state structures (Skocpol,

1979, p. 41). All three countries were "well established imperial states" that broke down not because of revolutionary agitation but because the states were inadequate to meet military challenges. This circumstance released political and class conflicts, and provided opportunities for leaders to mobilize the masses, although structural explanations emphasize "objective" contradictions, not the will of the revolutionists. The new states created by these social revolutions, Skocpol argues, were more powerful and more autonomous than the previous regimes, and peasants and workers were more directly incorporated—suggesting, against the conventional view, that peasants need not fare worse under totalitarian regimes than under other forms (Skocpol, 1979, pp. 286–291).

BEYOND THE BOURGEOISIE

Skocpol's analysis is in fundamental contrast with the classic Marxist approach to revolution, which centers on advanced capitalist development and the crucial role of the bourgeoisie, which was supposed to bring about the first of the necessary revolutions on the road to socialism. *States and Social Revolutions* rather gives primary importance to the dynamics of the peasant and agrarian economies of France, Russia, and China. "The fundamental politically relevant tensions in all three Old Regimes were not between commercial-industrial classes and landed aristocracies" but "were centered in the relationships of producing classes to the dominant classes and states, and in the relationships of the landed dominant classes to the autocratic-imperial states" (Skocpol, 1979, p. 48). While the upper landed classes and the state were "partners in the control and exploitation of the peasantry," they were also competitors in controlling the peasantry and appropriating the surpluses; this did not necessarily preclude reform (as the cases of Prussia and Japan showed), but according to Skocpol, in the cases she studied, reform did not occur because of the excessive strength of the landed aristocracy (Skocpol, 1979, pp. 49–50).

The crises that Skocpol presents as determinative in causing social revolutions were also predominantly agrarian: a table comparing the author's three focal countries in contrast to Prussia, Japan, and England shows that outside pressures on the states did not correlate with revolutions, nor did the presence of a strong bureaucracy. Only the agrarian nature of the Skocpol revolutions and the capitalist or transitional nature of the others distinguished the two groups (Skocpol, 1979, p. 155).

Yet the collapse of old regimes did not necessarily, of itself, solve the problem of why certain sociopolitical arrangements replaced them; this problem led to Skocpol's innovative attention to state building. Assuming that the "goal" of the nation's political process is "full state bureaucratization and direct mass political incorporation" (Skocpol, 1979, p. 161), and that leaders are actors "struggling to assert and make good their claims to state sovereignty" (Skocpol, 1979, p. 164), Skocpol describes the mid-revolutionary interregnum as a struggle over fundamental national issues, using the circumstances that particularly existed, "until relatively stable new state organizations have been consolidated" (Skocpol, 1979, p. 165).

But it is important to her argument that these political leaders 'do not know what they are doing,' that their ideologies and political intentions are irrelevant to political outcomes. While ideologies are useful tools for rallying elites and mobilizing masses, they do not "predict" the outcomes of the state building process, which for Skocpol is instead guided "by existing structural conditions" and the "rapidly changing currents of revolutions," and often ends up accomplishing quite different tasks from those it started with (Skocpol, 1979, pp. 170–171).

> *Revolutionary crises are not total breakpoints in history that suddenly make anything at all possible if only it is envisaged by willful revolutionaries! . . . revolutionary crises have particular forms, and create specific concatenations of possibilities and impossibilities, according to how these crises are originally generated in given old regimes under given circumstances. Furthermore, although a revolutionary crisis does entail institutional breakdowns and class conflicts that quickly change the parameters of what is possible in the given society, many conditions—especially socioeconomic conditions—always "carry over" from the old regime. These, too, create specific possibilities and impossibilities within which revolutionaries must operate as they try to consolidate the new regime. And so do the given world-historical and international contexts within which the entire revolutionary transformation occurs" (Skocpol, 1979, p. 171).*

THE APPLICATION OF STRUCTURAL METHODS

The center of Skocpol's analytic argument is located in the three chapters where she discusses successively the French, Russian, and Chinese revolutions. Here one finds basically three national "stories" about the revolutions, and it is not always clear that the three cases are comparable or even parallel. The chapter on France emphasizes Skocpol's differences with the largely Marxist "social interpretation" of the French revolutions, based on the overthrow of feudalism and the aristocracy by the capitalist bourgeoisie. Skocpol replaces this theory with the book's state building approach (Skocpol, 1979, pp. 174–175). While she convincingly suggests that this bureaucratic interpretation of the French revolution clarifies the distinction between the French case and the classic bourgeois revolutions such as the English, it never becomes clear that this French difference has been explained by Skocpol's recounting. Furthermore, the relevance of the Russian revolution to the French model is not vigorously shown: Despite the importance of peasant activity in the revolutionary period and the resulting political centralization, Skocpol herself describes the two revolutions as "qualitatively different," especially because of the role of the communist party and its orientation to a nationalized economy, and its more coercive authoritarianism (Skocpol, 1979, p. 206). By the time the story reaches China, which is said (Skocpol, 1979, p. 234) to be quite different from either France or Russia, the reader has begun to question the merits of the comparison itself. The analysis of the Chinese revolutionary period between 1911 and 1949 is, however, the jewel of Skocpol's analysis, and illustrates with depth and clarity her structural approach in its greatest strength.

The Chinese revolution seemed to distinguish itself from other revolutions both by its length and the complexity of the politics of which it was composed, pitting Chiang Kai-Shek's and Mao Tse-tung's forces in a long-running war of strange bedfellows and ambiguous allies. Skocpol begins the discussion of China's revolution with a description of the relatively underdeveloped state of the economy, except for modern destructive weaponry; and the "warlord" period's effect of radically weakening society both by its disorders and its absorption of civilian elements. This meant the revolution could not begin in society proper but only in the military system itself (Skocpol, 1979, pp. 238, 241).

Unlike the two other revolutions included in the book, the Chinese revolution had two parallel components, the Kuomintang and the Communists, both of which achieved considerable success, but in different social spheres—urban and rural, respectively. By 1927, the Kuomintang turned exclusively to "the financial resources of Chinese businesses" and to revenues from international trade and the Western powers; a choice that effectively precluded success in consolidating centralized state power because the resources were inadequate for political control and could not reach the village level where local forces maintained their sway (Skocpol, 1979, pp. 246–249).

STRUCTURE AND DECISION

The structural logic of the Kuomintang position controlled its options, according to Skocpol: Economic development investment was impossible because all Kuomintang funds were absorbed by administration, patronage, and military expenditure, and if the Japanese invasion had not occurred, the agrarian crisis would have undercut Kuomintang rule anyway. Their competitors, the communists, profited "by the same conditions that undermined the nationalists" because the communists had no other resource left but the peasants and circumstances forced the communists into policies of attention to and care of peasants, which would provide the core of a successful national-centralizing strategy (Skocpol, 1979, pp. 250–252).

With the Kuomintang controlling the cities and the communists entrenched in the countryside, the particular nature of "outside events" had a different impact upon each: for instance, the fact that the invading Japanese lacked the manpower to move into the rural areas. This meant that the urban KMT forces were forced into retreat, while the communists retained their strategic heartland and grew stronger. In addition, when the invasion caused thousands of students and intellectuals to flee the cities, the communists were prepared to welcome them to Yenan where they were trained as political, military, and administrative cadres for the party (Skocpol, 1979, pp. 257–258).

Based as it is on individual and group strategy as political choices occur in actual historical context, Skocpol's structuralism is therefore not the dehumanized play of vast social forces, but the specific interaction of conditions and human individuals. Certain "objective" forces occur at specific conjunctures, and these may favor or hamper individual leaders' strategies, and shape though not determine the political outcomes. But if in this way Skocpol's structuralism is a strong analytic tool, it also deliberately ignores important individual factors. This goes beyond the overly abstract debates between proponents of "structure" versus proponents of "culture" or ideological factors, and is more subtle.[9]

Skocpol at one point remarks that the Chinese communist leaders "recognized" what tactics they would have to use in a given situation; but she overlooks the case, surely of equal relevance, when leaders "fail to recognize" their opportunities or dangers, as presented by the circumstances. One need not be an advocate of "great men" theories of history to observe that if various Chinese leaders had missed their opportunities, or if France's military leaders had been blockheads unable to win battles, then the histories of her revolutions might have developed differently. Napoleon, Lenin, Mao, and other, lesser men need not make history, but history might often be different without them. This is one of the dangers of looking only at positive cases: for comparative purposes, *States and Social Revolutions* needs more revolutionary failures to allow the approach to yield its full lessons.

The state-building emphasis, bringing the state back in after the behavioralists had seemed to throw it out, was essentially a transitional movement; because it largely lacked any directive theory, the movement had nowhere to go once its original statement had been made. In almost every case, however, the structural-historical emphasis in books like Skocpol's had the effect of driving inquiry and research forward in a particular direction, toward an attempt to settle the state-society dichotomy by redefining all the elements now deemed relevant into a single micro-analytic but political and institutional base. But this did not emerge immediately.

This type of analysis of the state, as opposed to Marxist or Weberian rhetoric, opened an entirely new perspective on institutional behavior. It was not so much bringing the state back in as it was bringing circumstances, strategy, and politics back in. Others had earlier taken this route, and their work gained credence under the statist umbrella. Guillermo O'Donnell's work in Latin America (1988) was a prime example of the political approach to state analysis.

THE BUREAUCRATIC AUTHORITARIAN STATE

Comparative politics is regularly enriched at the analytic level by events in different areas of the world, events that are not in accord with conventional thinking among American political scientists. This was the case with dependency theory, which forced developmentalists to recognize that their self-centered, beneficent view of political and economic change was subject to less kindly interpretations. Another voice, from Latin

America, directed mainstream developmentalist attention to the state well before the state was officially brought back in; this was Guillermo O'Donnell's work on modernization and bureaucratic-authoritarianism in which he claimed that modernization in South America was associated not with progress but with a new type of authoritarianism, exemplified in Argentina, Brazil, Uruguay, and Chile (O'Donnell, 1988, p. xi).[10]

Bureaucratic-authoritarianism (BA) is often treated as a static conceptual term; the major question in such cases being whether the classification is sufficiently precise to use as a measuring tool. The more interesting question is how bureaucratic-authoritarianism actually works in practice, and the more lasting value of O'Donnell's work is the dynamic analysis he uses to probe the origins, the development, and the outcomes of the bureaucratic-authoritarian syndrome.[11]

O'Donnell begins with the by-now-accepted argument that Latin America was not underdeveloped in the usual senses of the term because nations were fully capitalist, although in a dependent form. Since the second world war the primary product export economy had changed into transnational corporation investment directly into the domestic market (because, incidentally, of the protectionist policies of Latin American nations). This change created, O'Donnell argues, a cluster of related imbalances: Latin American societies produced few of their own capital goods and little of their technology; services used in production were not usually generated locally; there was a positive balance of trade but not a positive balance of payments, since profits went abroad; domestic capital markets were weak; transnational corporation subsidiaries dominated the economy; there were severe inequalities in all resources; and goods and services reflected those of the core capitalist states (O'Donnell, 1988, p. 12).

These conditions created a foundation for the crises that produced the bureaucratic-authoritarian impetus: The basic problem was that the economy was not "normal." What is meant by normal? O'Donnell's answer illustrates his talent for being both specific in referent and general at the analytic level, as well as his willingness to deal with issues other theorists bypass. Making no attempt to decide what a normal economy might mean for some abstract economist, O'Donnell defines it from the viewpoint of the individual capitalist, for whom an economy is normal "when its dynamic reproduction or expansion takes place without major disruptions to capitalist accumulation, and in particular to the accumulation of its large economic entities" (O'Donnell, 1988, p. 15). Or, in other words, when businessmen feel perfectly confident of their ability to make a killing.

DEPARTURES FROM "NORMAL"

Capitalists must, he says, (1) enjoy rates of profit they find satisfactory, (2) reinvest profits sufficiently to stimulate growth, and (3) have the confidence that this will go on into the long-range future (O'Donnell, 1988, pp. 16–17). Where these conditions of "normalcy" break down, O'Donnell argues, a perverse type of economy is generated where instead of long-term investment the rule is short-run maximization—in other words, "plunder." While firms might continue to receive high profits, there would be pessimism rather than satisfaction; and there would be financial speculation, capital flight, and loss of capital inflow. Workers as well would turn to microrational plunder, having no reason to moderate their demands when everything was falling apart, the long-term future could not be counted upon, and in general, when there might be no tomorrow. As institutional and ideological controls became irrelevant, behavior became chaotic (O'Donnell, 1988, pp. 20–21).

O'Donnell then shows how this general pattern worked itself out in Argentina, Brazil, Chile, and Uruguay in a series of economic and political crises. First of all, the countries' economies were not "normal": There were severe fluctuations in economic growth, large intersectoral transfers of income, high and rising inflation with strong fluctuations, recurrent balance of payments crises, suspension of direct investment and credit from abroad, and so on. Along with the economic crisis came political crisis, with the expansion of an urban-based popular sector including a rapidly growing working class concentrated by the type of industrialization taking place, and the increasing weight of this class in the political arena.

Conflict in the political arena did not in these cases resolve itself, according to O'Donnell's analysis, but strengthened the activation of the various sectors, resulting in political turmoil and "mass praetorianism," where conflict was increasingly beyond any control and there was a fear that capitalism itself would be eliminated. The "state" in these nations had an extremely low level of autonomy with respect to all classes and became a battleground for the competing micro-rationalities it could not reconcile with normal economic functioning. O'Donnell argues that this led to a series of crises that followed with political logic one upon the other (O'Donnell, 1988, pp. 22–24).

Government crisis, as O'Donnell defines it, involves political instability, with a parade of high officials prematurely forced from office, accompanied by erratic changes in policy and a widespread feeling that no public power was possible. The state lost both legitimacy and majesty and was seen as nothing but a site of struggles by rival groups. More serious yet was the crisis of "regime" (the written and unwritten rules of the polity), where the various groups not only forced one another from office but tried to rewrite the rules governing political representation and who was allowed to hold office. O'Donnell argues that in Latin America these two crises can be endemic without substantially affecting economic performance, but when a third crisis occurs—the expansion of the political arena, which brings new participants into the process beyond what it can absorb—politics threatens to go beyond mere instability to loss of any control; rulers then become alarmed and try to put the subordinate classes back "in their place."

THE DYNAMICS OF CRISIS

Faced with restored exclusion from the arena, the dominated classes become rebellious and disorderly, threatening the bourgeoisie's claim to control the work process; this, says O'Donnell, is a deep crisis over the state as "guarantor of social domination" (O'Donnell, 1988, p. 26). Two subsequent crises may then follow: the attempt on the one hand to form a new social order, and/or the armed forces' taking over the state (O'Donnell, 1988, pp. 22–26). This final "crisis of hegemony" is based on an alliance of "order and authority."

> *The specificity of the BA in relation to other, past and present, authoritarian states in Latin America lies in this defensive reaction by the dominant classes and their allies to crises involving a popular sector that has been politically activated and is increasingly autonomous with respect to the dominant classes and the state apparatus" (O'Donnell, 1988, p. 31).*

In light of this dramatic panorama of the social, economic, and political events that may create the bureaucratic-authoritarian state, its specific characteristics do not stand in classificatory isolation but are seen as the result of and response to a complex social dynamic. The principal base of the bureaucratic-authoritarian state, according to O'Donnell's summary, is the upper bourgeoisie, the oligopolized and transnational class connected with global society; without this group the "specialists in coercion" (O'Donnell, 1988, pp. 31–33) have decisive weight.

The regime's principal strategy is to exclude from political effectiveness the previously active popular forces, using strict controls on participation, coercion, and the suppression of citizenship and democracy. All this is done in the name of "depoliticization," with political issues handed over to supposed neutral parties who use technical rationality as a means of suppression. Access to the governmental process becomes restricted to those who stand at the apex of large public and private organizations, especially the armed forces, businesses, and the civil bureaucracy (O'Donnell, 1988, pp. 31–32).

The response to O'Donnell's work has too often been to focus on his conclusions rather than his far more important method of analysis. What is scientifically interesting in O'Donnell's account is less the definition of bureaucratic authoritarianism and more the attempt to unravel the inner web of relationships that underlie the political processes of which bureaucratic authoritarianism was composed, from its preconditions, to its emergence, to its operation, and to its decline. In the discussion of these social, economic, and political relationships, O'Donnell employs the approach already encountered in such comparativists as Huntington, Moore, and Wallerstein, an approach centered on actual historical interactions of discrete individuals and groups. Here "the state" is not one black box facing another black box called "society"; here instead are recognizable political actors pursuing individual goals under compelling external circumstances. This appreciation of historical specificity grew because methods that sought grand universal explanations increasingly failed to match real situations.

CONTINUITIES IN THE STUDY OF THE STATE

Students of comparative politics often evaluate the crises and instabilities of the Third World against the normally functioning western democracies, as if it were quite clear that the differences were well understood and their causes well defined. Following

O'Donnell's dynamic analysis of the departures of certain Latin American nations from these landmarks of democracy, it is instructive to turn to an analysis by two European political scientists, Jan-Erik Lane and Svante O. Ersson, of the nations comprising the western European community, *Politics and Society in Western Europe* (1987). The book shows convincingly that much of what we "know" about democratic states is either untestable or invalid. But it points beyond these barriers and defines new approaches to the state. Lane and Ersson begin with a discussion of political cleavages characteristic of the political sociology tradition, but combine this approach with attention to the state, its institutions, and their relation to the social forces with which they deal.[12] The authors use as their primary concept the idea of political and social stability, always a major theme with political sociologists, but they warn vigorously against the inadequacies of the term for empirical analysis—fundamentally on the rather obvious grounds that stability is so difficult either to define or identify, and even more difficult to explain.

Stability is not the same as the absence of change, Lane and Ersson contend, for stable government may include new policies, new political alignments, even major changes in decision rules. A better approach identifies stability with adaptation, which may be both active and passive in respect to new circumstances and challenges. The definitional problem is further complicated when one attempts to study "democratic stability," according to the authors, since it is not yet settled whether this means a stable democratic system (democracy prevails while all else collapses) or a system that is both stable, in some overall way, and also democratic (Lane and Ersson, 1987, pp. 23, 278). To order their discussion, Lane and Ersson break stability into several levels, from the government level, involving institutional durability; to the party level, the maintenance of party mechanisms; to the whole society level where it entails social order (Lane and Ersson, 1987, pp. 1–11).

The independent variables in their analysis include cleavages at the government, party, and society levels; decision-making mechanisms such as election systems and rules of representation; and actual party struggles. The authors' approach is to avoid the "standard" two extremes of crediting socioeconomic structure with deterministic force, or privileging completely autonomous institutions. They seek instead a middle route heavily committed to the empirical testing of some time-worn hypotheses of political sociology. The weight of the book's contribution is to demonstrate vividly how tenuous is our knowledge of the modern industrialized society and its political institutions; most of our intuitive beliefs prove unsatisfactory when actually put to the test.

There are a great many theories about political stability, as Lane and Ersson document: Almond's theory of cross-cutting social cleavages leading to consensus and stability; Dahl's theory that polyarchy depends on social homogeneity and economics; Lijphart's theory that the decision-making structure of consociationalism leads to stability; the Sartori and Duverger theories that emphasize the role of the party system in stability; corporatist theory based upon importance of elite behavior; and so on (Lane and Ersson, 1987, Ch. 1). Simple tests based on measurements of instability (which is used because the absence of stability seems easier to measure than stability itself), are undercut by the "frequency fallacy," which involves the assumption that the same actions mean the same thing in different countries, that identical frequencies of an event connote identical levels of instability.

Lane and Ersson express the hope that the problem of equating events that may have different meanings can be at least moderated by restricting comparisons within a single region such as Western Europe (Lane and Ersson, 1987, p. 298), but of course the problem is a devastating barrier to the simple numerical comparisons upon which empiricists have based so much reliance. In one case, for instance, indicators showed countries as different as Italy, Greece, Portugal, and Finland as unstable; and the authors conclude that different countries tend to different styles of protest behavior, a conclusion that seriously weakens the assumption that stability indicators are universal and comparable (Lane and Ersson, 1987, p. 291).

POLITICAL CLEAVAGE ANALYSIS

Politics and Society in Western Europe has the particular virtue of summarizing hard-headedly a large body of earlier and current thought on the issues of democracy and stability; the result is to show how little the western world knows about the mechanisms by which it is governed and perhaps also how ill prepared are western political scientists to give concrete advice to the rest of the world. Using a traditional "structural" approach, the authors look first at contention among individuals and organizations as the primary dynamic force in society, and on the political system's function in reconciling conflicting interests. The specific cleavages in a society determine the patterns of conflict; sifting through a long list of possibly relevant cleavages, Lane and Ersson settle on religion, ethnicity, class and region as the most important (1987, p. 46).

In each case, however, the problem is that structural differences did not necessarily lead to the consciousness of cleavage among actual people, and if groups are not aware that their differences are relevant to political behavior, cleavages cannot be much of a force. This represents a difficulty especially for a structural view of political parties, which political sociologists have traditionally seen as based on objective interests rather than personalities or issues, and which serve as intermediaries with the state (Lane and Ersson, 1987, p. 97). But the relations between structural groups and political parties in Western Europe have not been as simple as usually thought, Lane and Ersson conclude; and parties that want to govern are often "catch all" parties. This makes it inappropriate to use parties as an indicator of stability (Lane and Ersson, 1987, pp. 125–130).

When it comes to studying party systems, the particular configuration of parties within a given country, furthermore, it turns out that all party systems are different (Lane and Ersson, 1987, p. 177). Again, this illustrates the minefields present in studying states and institutions: Comparability fails because truly crossnational variables are lacking. Lane and Ersson use fractionalization, functional orientation, polarization, radicalization, and volatility to define party systems; the results showed lack of stability, although stability increased in the post-world war two period. Yet fluctuations and trends had apparently no correlation, according to the authors' data (Lane and Ersson, 1987, pp. 177–179). Once more, the apparently straightforward notion of stability proved empirically elusive.

STATE AND CITIZEN AUTONOMY

These preliminaries having been dispatched, *Politics and Society in Western Europe* takes up issues of statehood and autonomy, using autonomy in a novel manner as a concept that refers both to the political system and its members, so that autonomy becomes not a simple dichotomy (present or not present) but an empirical dimension measuring the degree of influence distribution between institutions and individuals over political policies (Lane and Ersson, 1987, pp. 180–181). The study of state decision-making structures assumes that the way decisions are handled affects the capacity of citizens and organizations to influence government, and to affect policy outcomes. This is a staple assumption of both traditional and behavioral approaches to political systems, but Lane and Ersson argue it is an open question whether different governmental mechanisms actually matter (1987, p. 211).

They present a tentative theory of the types of political structure: (1) mass influence systems, based on referenda and proportionality; (2) elite influence systems such as consociationalism and corporatism; and (3) cabinet influence systems (Lane and Ersson, 1987, pp. 251–252). Comparability and testability here again fail, however, since the issue-making and issue-resolving process varied across the European nations studied, and political problem management was a function of the particular problems a particular nation happened to encounter during its historical progress (Lane and Ersson, 1987, p. 258).

Lane and Ersson review the fifteen European nations on the types of issue important for each. Italy, for instance, was characterized by two basic issues, labor-capital and religion-secularism; Belgium by structural issues of religion and language; Sweden by lack of cleavage; and so on (Lane and Ersson, 1987, pp. 259–271). The roots of democratic stability and the role of state structures remain elusive, given this diversity. Yet in one sense, this negative conclusion is itself a contribution to the debate: Too many scholars assume our understanding of these matters is self-evident and satisfactory, where Lane and Ersson systematically have shown how many gaping holes remain in our knowledge of our own democratic political systems.

POST-MODERNISM AND THE STATE

If, as someone has said, deconstruction and post-modernism are the last refuge of those who are bored with reality, this may explain why such analysis has been relatively rare among students of comparative politics, who have too much unfinished empirical and theoretical business to find boredom a problem. The objective of the deconstructionist school is to take apart conventional entities and show that they are illusory. This sometimes goes so far that reality begins to float freely somewhere high above the heads of normal folks. But to ignore deconstruction is sometimes to be guilty of swallowing unexamined concepts whole. This suggestion was the gravamen of an intriguing article in the august pages of *The American Political Science Review* (Mitchell, 1991) that serves to close this discussion of some highlights of the state literature and point the way to more recent approaches in comparative politics. Mitchell's basic argument is simple: that if one is to use the state as a conceptual term, then one should be able to define it, which means basically distinguishing the state from society; but in fact the boundary between the two is "elusive, porous, and mobile." Reference is in this respect made to Schmitter's blithe definition of the state as "an amorphous complex of agencies with ill-defined boundaries performing a great variety of not very distinctive functions" (Mitchell, 1991, p. 77).

Mitchell argues that the original behavioralists abandoned the concept of the state as being too vague, but found that defining the "system" was no easier. The second solution to the difficulty of defining the state was to separate it entirely from social forces, making it an autonomous entity with its own voluntarist will. The alternative approach taken by Mitchell's article is to eschew absolute definitions of some clear line between state and society, and to ask "in a given area of practice, how is the effect created that certain aspects of what occurs pertains to society, while others stand apart as the state" (Mitchell, 1991, p. 89).

The exemplary case presented by Mitchell is taken from Krasner's study of the relation between the United States government and the Arabian American Oil Company, a consortium of major U.S. oil companies with exclusive rights to Saudi oil. When after world war two the Saudis demanded an increase in royalties from 12 percent to 50 percent, ARAMCO (wishing neither to lose its profits nor raise its prices) and the U.S. State Department (anxious to subsidize the pro-American Saudis) arranged through a loophole in the U.S. tax laws that the royalty was treated "as if" it were a direct foreign tax, to be paid not from company profits but from the taxes ARAMCO owed the U.S. Treasury. The royalty, Mitchell says, was "paid not by the company but by U.S. taxpayers," so that the distinction between state and society was difficult to draw. The Saudis, ARAMCO, the State Department, and U.S. taxpayers were all happy with the situation—the latter, presumably, in their ignorance (Mitchell, 1991, p. 89).

What creates the "state," Mitchell contends, is the organizations created by social and political negotiations that are ongoing over time. The military, for instance, takes on its state-related reality because it builds barracks and other installations; we can see the buildings, so we invent the state as a summary term—and fail to notice how quickly new organizations may move in and out of the buildings. The state, according to Mitchell, is the metaphysical effect of social practices, not a structure; and its boundaries are not real edges. States should be seen "as an effect of detailed processes of spatial organization, temporal arrangement, functional specification, and supervision and surveillance" that create the appearance of a world divided into state and society (Mitchell, 1991, pp. 94–95). Such a perspective is only apparently radical, since more empirically oriented political scientists were moving toward a similar accord on the idea that microanalysis of social events, from peasant revolutions to state institutions, was the next step in the intellectual progress of comparative politics.

CONCLUSION

Students of comparative politics can derive several lessons from "the return to the state." On the one hand, the journey showed once again the difficulty of developing explanatory theory. Arguments over the meaning of state autonomy or state capacity replaced research-oriented theory and were sterile—the debates provided no assistance at all to researchers who needed to have some guidance into the types of data they should collect and the causal connections they should investigate. On the other hand, bringing the state back in did encourage a reconsideration of political factors that were important but had been rigorously ignored by the proponents of systems theories and the socially based empirical techniques. This return of "politics" would mark the next phase of the comparative politics search, the investigation of state-society relations and the new institutionalism.

NOTES

1. Churchland, for instance, makes a major issue of the everyday misperception that the sun "rises" rather than that the earth turns. He recommends a re-education of the senses by turning the head to the right when facing the setting sun or moon, so that their ecliptic is horizontal in the visual field. With a little practice, he suggests, one can learn to see the universe as we know it actually is, with the stars "motionless" around the turning earth (Churchland, 1979, pp. 30–34). Of course one may acquire only a twisted neck; but Churchland's argument about our tranquil capacity to "see things wrongly" is certainly correct.

2. The larger role of the Social Science Research Council in American social science is discussed in Sibley (1974), and criticized in Fisher (1993). Its influence was central to developments in comparative politics in both the behavioral and post-behavioral periods.

3. The chapters included in the *Bringing the State Back In* volume are illustrative of the practical interests of the contributors: a partial sample includes Charles Tilly, "War Making and State Making as Organized Crime"; Peter Katzenstein, "Small Nations in an Open International Economy; The Converging Balance of State and Society in Switzerland and Austria"; David D. Laitin, "Hegemony and Religious Conflict: British Imperial Control and Political Cleavages in Yorubaland."

4. Comparative politics has often defined its research options in terms of a sharp distinction between "scientific" approaches based on correlational studies between quantitative variables on the one hand, and on the other hand, case studies that were seen as thoroughly unscientific, albeit full of rich and interesting information. While the "scientific" school took the leadership position during the behavioral period, thoughtful advocates of the case method argued that if the method was combined with explicit attempts at theory development, the case

method could serve equally well in the development of comparative theory. See, for instance, Eckstein (1975).

5. Hegel's philosophy was constructed according to a metaphysical position usually called idealism (though the term is not quite accurate for Hegel). Its basic premise was that ideas were the guiding force of history. This allowed Hegel and others to argue that a nation-state might at a given point in history represent the highest form of human freedom, even if some of its citizens were in miserable condition. Rising above such mundane problems, Hegel's state was "the actuality of the ethical Idea" and "absolutely rational" (Hegel, 1952, p. 155). The *Philosophy of Right*, while antithetical to American political thought, repays acquaintance. A useful guide to a complex thinker is Kaufmann (1965).

6. Anyone who wishes to appreciate this search for theory should consult some of the original sources. See, for Marx, "The Contribution to the Critique of Hegel's Philosophy of Right," "The Paris Manuscripts," "The German Ideology," "The Eighteenth Brumaire," "The Civil War in France," and Volume One of *Das Kapital*, which is more readable and on occasion more amusing than the reader might expect. Many of these writings are usefully included in Tucker (1978). Weber's works have been widely published, but in fragmented versions. An accessible introduction is Bendix (1960).

7. A comparable analysis of viewpoints on the Development State (Onis, 1991) attends less to the political dynamics and more to the political structure of developing regimes, in this case in the East Asian region.

8. Interest in the study of revolution has fluctuated widely over recent decades, as have the methods used. Gurr's theory of relative deprivation (1970) has been the most methodologically advanced; systems approaches (Johnson, 1966) have proceeded without benefit of quantitative data. The basic fallacy of revolutionary theory is to overemphasize a transient phenomenon (revolutionary activity) and pay insufficient attention to the structural underpinnings that explain the society in its "normal" operations.

9. Skocpol's well-known debate with the cultural forces, published initially in 1985 in the *Journal of Modern History*, is reprinted in Skocpol (1994), Chapters 7 and 8.

10. The work was initially reported in O'Donnell (1973).

11. An important collection of papers on bureaucratic authoritarianism is Collier (1979).

12. It is useful to compare Lane and Ersson's rigorously positivist approach to the data in political sociology to such early works as that of Lipset (discussed in Chapter 2 above).

REFERENCES

Bendix, Reinhard. *Max Weber: An Intellectual Portrait*. New York: Doubleday Anchor, 1960.

Brierly, J. S. *The Law of Nations*. New York: Oxford University Press, 1963.

Chilcote, Ronald H. *Theories of Comparative Politics*. Boulder: Westview Press, 1994.

Churchland, P. M. *Scientific Realism and Plasticity of Mind*. Cambridge: Cambridge University Press, 1979.

Collier, David (Ed.). *The New Authoritarianism in Latin America*. Princeton: Princeton University Press, 1979.

Eckstein, Harry. "Case Study and Theory in Political Science." In Fred I. Greenstein and Nelson W. Polsby (Eds.). *Handbook of Political Science* (Volume 7, Chapter 3, pp. 79–137). Reading: Addison Wesley, 1975.

Evans, P. *Dependent Development: The Alliance of Multinational, State, and Local Capital.* Princeton: Princeton University Press, 1979.

Evans, Peter B. "Foreign Capital and the Third World State." (Originally in Evans, Rueschemeyer and Skocpol). In Myron Weiner and Samuel P. Huntington, *Understanding Political Development* (pp. 319–352). Glenview: Little Brown, 1987.

Evans, Peter B., Dietrich Rueschemeyer, and Theda Skocpol (Eds.). *Bringing the State Back In.* New York: Cambridge University Press, 1985.

Fisher, Donald. *Fundamental Development of the Social Sciences: Rockefeller Philanthropy and the United States Social Science Research Council.* Ann Arbor: University of Michigan Press, 1993.

Giere, Ronald N. *Explaining Science: A Cognitive Approach.* Chicago: University of Chicago Press, 1988.

Gurr, Ted Robert. *Why Men Rebel.* Princeton: Princeton University Press, 1970.

Hegel, G. W. F. *Hegel's Philosophy of Right* (Trans. T. M. Knox). London: Oxford University Press, 1952.

Hilton, Denis J. (Ed.). *Contemporary Science and Natural Explanation: Commonsense Conceptions of Causality.* New York: New York University Press, 1988.

Huntington, Samuel P. *Political Order in Changing Societies.* New Haven: Yale University Press, 1968.

Johnson, Chalmers A. *Revolutionary Change.* Boston: Little Brown, 1966.

Kaufmann, Walter. *Hegel: A Reinterpretation.* New York: Doubleday Anchor, 1965.

Lane, Jan-Erik, and Svante O. Ersson. *Politics and Society in Western Europe.* Newbury Park: Sage, 1987 (Second Edition, 1991).

Lijphart, Arendt. *Democracy in Plural Societies.* New Haven: Yale University Press, 1977.

Mitchell, Timothy. "The Limits of the State: Beyond Statist Approaches." *American Political Science Review* LXXX, no. 1 (March 1991): 77–96.

O'Donnell, Guillermo. *Modernization and Bureaucratic Authoritarianism.* Berkeley: Institute of International Studies, University of California at Berkeley, 1973.

O'Donnell, Guillermo. *Bureaucratic Authoritarianism: Argentina 1966–1973 in Comparative Perspective.* Berkeley: University of California Press, 1988.

Onis, Ziya. "The Logic of the Developmental State (Review Article)." *Comparative Politics* 24, no. 1 (October 1991): 109–126.

Sibley, Elbridge. *Social Science Research Council: The First Fifty Years.* New York: Social Science Research Council, 1974.

Skocpol, Theda. *States And Social Revolutions.* New York: Cambridge University Press, 1979.

Skocpol, Theda. *Social Revolutions In The Modern World.* Cambridge: Cambridge University Press, 1994.

Tucker, Robert C. (Ed.) *The Marx-Engels Reader* (Second Edition). New York: W. W. Norton, 1978.

Weiner, Myron, and Samuel P. Huntington. *Understanding Political Development.* Glenview: Little Brown, 1987.

5

State and Society and the New Institutionalism

METHODS OF ANALYTIC INSTITUTIONALISM

Every science must, if it is to make sustained progress, find its bottom, the basic unit of analysis from which it will work and upon which it will build. Achieving this foundation is often easier said than done, however, and the work of comparative politics traced so far bears testimony to the difficulties. Traditional political scientists thought the basic unit was government, in the abstract and without inconvenient human inhabitants. The behavioralist revolution made a radical shift to using individuals as the basic political unit, but these individuals were defined in isolation both from government and from politics. This was what the critics of behavioralism had in mind when they claimed the approach was "reductionist," that it reduced political individuals so far that they lost the very traits that made them interesting. Survey research also fell under this stricture, when verbal responses proved unreliable, and there was no way to test whether opinions actually affected political actions.

The return to the state seemed a swing of the pendulum back to the traditional emphasis on government, but since no discipline can exactly repeat its past, the state approach had to take account of the behavioral period that intervened. So when scholars looked at the state this time, it had people in it, and the state was not just the constitution and the laws but agencies and institutions, administrators and officials, real people with real goals and tactics of their own. The return to the state, therefore, led to the breaking up of the state into analytic pieces—and once this was done, it was obvious the observer could no longer talk about the state, but only really about the various groups and coalitions that made it up. And when that was settled, it was furthermore clear that the individuals, groups, and coalitions would not be always in agreement.

This discovery brought comparative politics research into the 1990s, with several somewhat different approaches tending to converge into an agreement that it was important to look at behavior at the grassroots of the political system, and to see the individuals there as highly influenced by a complex structure made up of social, economic, and political institutions, within which they designed their lives, careers, and their politics as best they could, occasionally changing some institutions to adapt better to their needs and desires, but constrained by other individuals who might prefer things to be left alone. There is as yet no settled label for this movement, which includes research into peasant communities, into intragovernmental politics, into the interrelations between state and society, and into various forms of the new institutionalism.

For convenience I refer to this period in comparative politics as that of analytic institutionalism, an approach that defines institutions in terms of the people who make, sustain, or change them, and focuses on the political process by which this occurs. That there is much tacit agreement among students of comparative politics on this approach to their subject matter is evidence for the argument that the discipline has progressed scientifically and arrived at a workable framework for scientific research in the present period.

The discussion begins with two students of the peasant village who engaged in a debate over what went on in such villages, which showed vividly how theory shapes perception. It then goes on to a work that used the peasant experience to develop insights that led to a general model of state-society behavior, and to neoinstitutionalism in two forms. A final summary draws together the basic precepts of the analytic institutionalism model.

BRINGING THE PEASANT VILLAGE IN

James C. Scott's *The Moral Economy of the Peasant* (1976) is among those rare works that while complex in purpose and in methodology nonetheless achieve a classic simplicity of theme: For most political scientists the book was their first full introduction to "the peasant" as a real person with real problems, real cultural roots, and a coherent way of life. Until this time it is fair to say most persons who had not specialized in peasant studies considered peasants either in Lerner's light as speeding into the economic and political future as fast as they could escape their villages; or in a structural-functional light as the benighted "traditionalists" who were maintaining their backwardness in the teeth of the world's encouragement toward achieving modernity. Scott's invitation to meet the peasant therefore came as a revelation.

Proceeding with a phenomenological viewpoint, from American social psychology, with an acquaintance with the French *Annales* historians and their interest in enduring social structures, and with economists such as Polanyi who emphasized precapitalist economic relations (Scott, 1976, p. 5), Scott attempted to present peasant economies and life structures from the peasants' own point of view. In light of subsequent criticism of his moral economy approach, it is interesting to remark how deep was Scott's concern to show that apparently inexplicable peasant behavior was in fact sensible, straightforward, and rational, given the particular problems the peasant communities faced. Many of the themes characteristic of contemporary analytic institutionalism are combined in Scott's book—the microanalytic approach, the emphasis on the physical environment in which choices are made, the recognition of the state participants as negotiating actors rather than absolute forces, the sense of all these factors combined in the creation of informal but strong institutional structures.

Scott began his analysis with a metaphor from the economist Tawney, of the peasant represented by a man standing up to his neck in water so that even the smallest wave may put him under completely (Scott, 1976, p. 1). While Scott's primary focus was Southeast Asian peasants, the implications of his analysis extended to all hard-pressed peasant societies, in medieval Europe or in the present. This illustrates that microanalysis, though unlike grand systems theories, may equally achieve universality and open new dimensions for comparison as a method.

Looked at from the drowning man perspective, the peasant appeared to Scott as pursuing a primary life strategy of "safety first," minimizing the "subjective probability of the maximum loss." Such an assumption made explicable the apparent "irrationalities" of peasant behavior—such as the use of more than one seed variety or of farming scattered strips rather than larger more efficient areas—as well as the practices of maintaining communal or common land for redistribution or use as circumstances necessitated, and the frequent peasant norms that enjoined charity on all (Scott, 1976, pp. 4–5). Peasants who are risk-averse rather than vigorous capitalist entrepreneurs may not fit the economists' preconceptions, Scott argued, but such peasants are nonetheless rational, given the conditions of their lives, which are too near the margins of starvation to gamble on speculative profits which, if they fail, lead to immediate hunger and death—and here Scott provided some fearsome examples of peasant famines throughout history.

PRACTICAL VALUE SYSTEMS

The "moral economy" postulated by Scott had two major dimensions. First, there was the peasant axiom that every member of the community had a right to a subsistence level of existence, a subsistence defined in terms of what local conditions permit (not "living well" but at least a meal a day, for example), and what were seen to be the "cultural decencies" of having sufficient resources, say, to marry off one's children or properly bury one's dead. Included in this subsistence norm, according to Scott, was social pressure on the well-off to help the worse off; peasants are not egalitarians, Scott emphasized, and do not expect income leveling; but there must be, for everyone, what modern societies call the safety net, the point below which no one shall be forced to endure.

Based on the rule of subsistence was a second rule, reciprocity, a rule of inter-personal conduct that held that one should help, or at least not hurt, those who help him; or, more specifically, a gift or a service creates an obligation to return something of comparable value. When this rule operated between unequals it created patron-client relationships where the well-to-do gave money, food, or assistance when needed, and the poor man turned up at his patron's side "if there was a showdown" (Scott, 1976, p. 42). In this social relation there may be wide cultural variation, Scott argued, but not utter relativity of values; there was, in short, a moral economy (Scott, 1976, pp. 167–179).

Such norm systems are not Kantian, according to Scott, for they are not based upon internal moral imperatives; rather such norm systems work "in large measure through the abrasive force of gossip and envy and the knowledge that the abandoned poor are likely to be a real and present danger to better-off villagers" (Scott, 1976, pp. 5, 41). It is therefore incorrect to accuse Scott, as some critics have done, of building an idealistic moral economy for the peasants. Whatever are the norms, they are socially (and politically) created, maintained, and enforced.

Because Scott's central concern was with peasant rebellion, it was important for him to understand just what it is that causes outrage, anger, and violence in such communities. His argument here was contrary to what most outsiders seem to expect. Rather than making their judgments on the degree to which they are ("objectively") exploited, Scott argued that peasants judged not on the abstract justice of their situation but merely on whether, when all the exactions had been made by state and landlord, enough was left for the peasant and his family to live on until the next harvest. This implied "that a rent of 40 percent of the crop in a good year is likely to meet a less explosive resistance than a rent of 20 percent after a particularly poor year" (Scott, 1976, p. 29). Peasants' need for subsistence, year after year, underlies this behavior, according to Scott, as it does the constant negotiation and renegotiation between landholders and peasants over what system of risk distribution will be employed in their contracts.

In traditional, feudal land tenure systems, the landlord took all the risk—and took all the profits. The peasant cultivator was guaranteed a minimal fixed return for his service, and families were guaranteed their subsistence; this maximized their security. At the other end of the spectrum was fixed rent tenantry, where the landlord's return was guaranteed and the peasant cultivator got both the profit—and the risk. In between stood sharecropping where each got a proportion of both profit and risk (Scott, 1976, table, p. 45). However exploitative the relationships were, Scott said, peasants rarely blamed the system for their troubles; instead they blamed individual landlords who enforced contracts too strictly, failing to take into account drought or other agrarian difficulties (Scott, 1976, pp. 50–51).

As colonial pressures forced landowners to realize higher profits, and where peasants were strong enough to resist, the traditional struggle between the two groups surfaced in such devices as the "landlord's basket" used to measure crop payments: some baskets "were constructed so as to balloon out as they received rice, others were shaped to prevent leveling and ensure a heaping basket, certain methods of pouring increased the basket's capacity, and if it were shaken vigorously several times as it was filled, it would hold more" (Scott, 1976, p. 71). Marx's footnotes in *Das Kapital* on the children sleeping under their machines could not be more vivid testimony to an exploitative way of life.

THE ROLE OF THE STATE

The state entered these local struggles only belatedly, according to Scott's analysis, after colonialism and post-colonial national development occurred, because while the traditional state "did not have the means to impose its will" on village localities, the newer states did so. In the old days when exactions became too stringent, "subjects fled, black markets circumvented state monopolies, villages faked records and pleaded poverty," and taxes were simply not paid (Scott, 1976, p. 93). What the colonial order taught rulers was the need for "paperwork": "the inexorable progress of cadastral surveys, settlement reports for land revenue, censuses, the issuance of land titles and licenses, identity cards, tax rolls and receipts, and a growing body of regulations and procedures. . . . Nets of finer and finer official weave caught and recorded . . . each activity that was assessable" (Scott, 1976, p. 94).

At the village level, where the villagers believed that the ideal condition was to have no state at all, the colonial exactions were made worse by the local notables who were charged with collecting taxes and "frequently collected more than was due and pocketed the difference" (Scott, 1976, p. 109). When the great depression of the 1930s struck Southeast Asia, some peasants were goaded into despair and rebellion against states who still wanted to collect their usual taxes even though peasants were starving. But even rebellion depended very daintily on specific circumstances. In northern Annam, for instance, Scott argued that the most rebellious provinces had clayier soil that was "far more sensitive to variations in rainfall than sandy soils," and that drought in these cases caused greater hardship than in more stable areas nearby, a fact obscured by the statisticians' practice of averaging soil conditions within large districts (p. 140). As to why peasants did not revolt, given the almost universal exploitation they faced, Scott emphasized the peasant's willingness to utilize a wide variety of adaptive behaviors "that, for a time at least, stave off the immediate threat to subsistence"—they may find part-time labor, take up banditry, make crafts (pp. 194–195). Or, of course, the peasants may migrate to cities and enter the modern economy (p. 213).

MORAL OR POLITICAL ECONOMY

Evaluation of Scott's moral economy approach to peasant behavior requires attention to a subtle inconsistency in the argument, involving the meaning and origin of the social norm systems he describes. On the one hand, using the "drowning man" metaphor, the peasants' moral economy can be seen as a rational response to the peculiar circumstances of severe rural poverty and the uncertainty of harvests. Observing the negotiations of landlord, state, and peasant over who will get the profits and who will bear the risks, Scott's work fits easily into many versions of the economic approach. Tenants give themselves into the clutches of the landlord only, according to Scott, because of the hope that if bad times come, the landlord will help them and thus allow them to avert starvation.

The peasant attachment to "tradition" is, from this viewpoint, not emotional so much as based on an empirical belief that custom is likely to increase the landlord's compliance with the contract he has made (Scott, 1976, p. 179). In fact, Scott's peasants have solved, with their moral economy structures, the well-known dilemma of the prisoners, where persons who would benefit from cooperation fail to do so because each cannot trust the other to take the necessary cooperative action, given that the other cannot trust the first.[1] "Moral" behavior is therefore well within the economic framework: If insurance is a rational hedge against uncertainty, then so too are peasant norms. But the "rational" argument often drifts into a justification of the moral economy for its own value, independent of its immediate utility, and here Scott left himself open to criticism.

THE PEASANT AS CLASSIC ECONOMIC MAN

In launching his "political economy" attack on the moral economy school (in *The Rational Peasant,* 1979), Samuel Popkin set up a strawman against which to compare his own preferred method, by making for his opponents' claims much stronger than those they made for themselves. "Moral economists have argued that, from the perspective of peasant welfare, peasant society is moral, economically efficient, and stable" (Popkin, 1979, p. 29). While this was an excessive claim, Popkin's general point was clearly valid, when he argued that "moral economists take too benign a view of villages and patron-client ties and too harsh a view of market potential" (ibid.). Popkin raised a series of points that delineate the kinds of questions that moral economists fail to answer (pp. 16–18).

- How are village norms derived?
- What determines the minimal subsistence level?
- How are competing claims assessed and resources distributed?
- How are needs assessed? Is "income averaging" allowable?
- Who works for whom, when work-sharing occurs?
- Are "need" and "inability to pay" the same?
- How are the results of laziness distinguished from acts of fate?
- Can someone contributing to another today be sure of repayment?
- What is an enforceable norm?
- Under what conditions do individuals break norms?

The raising of such questions has the effect of pulling off the cover of a jar and finding that ants have gotten into the pickled peaches. Where Scott tended to see peasants as relatively united against landlord exactions, and cooperating in their "war against nature" with unpredictable weather and other natural forces, Popkin saw the village as a nest of distrusts, jealousies, frictions, and rivalries (Popkin, 1979, p. 17). And no matter how seriously the student has entertained the moral economy perspective, it is difficult to deny these negative aspects of small communities—especially for anyone who has ever lived in a small town.

Peasants' strategic calculations have two dimensions for Popkin: whether they are to invest their surplus in individual or family goods such as children (long-run insurance) and animals or land (short-run security); or whether they invest in village-wide insurance or welfare programs (Popkin, 1979, p. 19). Popkin argued that peasants prefer investment in individual goods, and would be quite willing to speculate on risky innovations if there was some security (pp. 21–22). Furthermore, he asked, in traditional political economy style, if there was a moral economy in the village, why would anyone work? This "free rider" problem—that where all benefit from a good, no individual will willingly contribute to its provision because the others will do it for him—also applied to irrigation, flood control, religious rites, killing tigers, and fighting fires, according to Popkin (p. 24).

The different approaches, moral economy versus political economy, have policy implications as well. If, as Popkin claimed moral economists contend, only rich peasants will innovate and gains will therefore remain private, then bureaucracy is necessary if peasants are to benefit at all. From Popkin's political economy viewpoint, overly sanguine views of peasant cooperation among moral economists led to what he considered false hopes for community development schemes; and he argued that the bureaucratic "solution" causes more stratification than it eliminates (p. 28).

Popkin's argument centered on the claim that "the calculations of peasants driven by motives of survival in a risky environment led not to subsistence floors and extensive villagewide insurance schemes, but to procedures that generated and enforced inequality within the village" (Popkin, 1979, p. 33). Against what he called "romantic theories" about peasant society, Popkin drew a picture of the village upper classes in a constant war on all fronts against the poor. While very restricted and easily definable categories of persons were usually granted assistance by the village ("the aged, widowed, and orphaned"), according to Popkin, in all other cases it was everyone for him- or herself. Far from getting tax relief in hard times, for instance, in Vietnam "peasants typically were expected by fellow villagers to pay their own taxes even if it meant selling or mortgaging land, entering into debt-slavery, or breaking up the family" (p. 41). Popkin also described, rather than a mutual-help society in villages, a constant battle between "insiders" and "outsiders," with insiders severely restricting the rights of land ownership, access to the courts, and other village benefits (pp. 43–46).

SOLITARY, POOR, NASTY, BRUTISH . . .

The corporate village did not itself provide welfare floors, Popkin argued; rather, what insurance existed was specific (funerals, births, weddings) and was confined to small groups of equals within the village. "Strict reciprocity" was the rule for such insurance schemes and other cooperative ventures as well; given the human propensity to shirk, any villager must be constantly reassured that he "receives exactly what he has put into the scheme" (Popkin, 1979, pp. 47–48). Popkin's political economy thesis of universal distrust is supplemented also by his example of interest rates in peasant societies, which are extremely high because of the ability of debtors to flee; for this reason, creditors often took hostages from the debtor's family or the peasant himself, in various forms of debt slavery (pp. 54–55).

Village leaders, rather than benign patriarchs, were the focus of sharp distrust, and indeed rightly so, according to Popkin. "Members of village councils everywhere can and do collude with one another to their common advantage and at the expense of the village. It is equally clear that officeholding is also often looked upon as a way to make money or at least to protect fortunes" (Popkin, 1979, p. 59). On the other hand, villagers often prefer to have wealthy men in office, since the well-off leader is seen as less likely to abscond with the village funds entrusted to them (pp. 60–61).

Instead of the moral economists' village community, Popkin described a highly competitive, stratified society, engaged not in Rousseau's tranquil pursuits but in a lively war of Hobbesian men, each trying to outmaneuver the others. As the epitome of such institutionalized distrust, Popkin presented the "bell tower" solution to the threat of theft. One of the constraints against innovation in crops, he contended, was that new crops were likely to create new hazards to those who grew them because the crops presented new vulnerabilities. English peasants in the thirteenth century, for instance, acknowledged the benefits of supplementary crops of peas and beans, which were recommended by their good dietary value, by their not requiring milling as did grain, by the ability to pick and eat them green, and by the short time in which enough could be gathered to feed the entire family.

The problem, however, was that plantings in the pea fields were tall enough to hide in, and the pea fields were apart from the other fields; this made theft easy, and because of the nature of the crop, convenient for the hungry. The solution to such problems was the bell tower: Peasants agreed that no one could be in the pea and bean fields except at specified hours marked by the ringing of the bell (rung by the village priest); "at all other hours, any person carrying legumes could be presumed by all to be a thief." But from a strict political economy point of view, can we trust the priest? No, Popkin cheerfully notes, but "how much can one person eat?"[2]

It would distort Popkin's *The Rational Peasant* to consider only its debate with the moral economists, for when he turned to his own research in Vietnam, which focused on the varying effectiveness of four collective action movements, (the Catholic church, two indigenous religious movements, and the Communists), his emphasis was methodologically wider and more innovative than a strict political economy approach would allow (Popkin, 1979, Chapter 5). Popkin showed in his discussion of French colonialism in Vietnam how oversimplified it was to consider the colonial process as the imposition of one political regime upon another; rather, colonial forces were welcomed by some groups in society, and resisted by other local groups. When, for instance, the French tried to control local bureaucrats by confiscating their land if French orders were not properly carried out, local leaders simply substituted landless peasants against whom the French had no recourse (p. 175). The highly complex mesh of political interaction among rich, poor, French, mandarins, and others, was used by Popkin to explain the development of social institutions in twentieth century Vietnam.

CONVERSION AND REBELLION

Popkin showed convincingly that "conversions," whether to religious or political movements, were stimulated by a wide variety of material and ideological factors that went well beyond simple economic self-interest. Catholicism's power in Vietnam, according to Popkin's analysis, came not only from its inherent message but from its provision of "science, cannon, European education" along with better welfare and insurance benefits, better adjudication of village disputes, and the church's ability to manipulate the bureaucracy for the benefit of its followers (Popkin, 1979, pp. 189–192). The Cao Dai, a popular religious movement, modeled itself on the Catholic model (except that its saints included Charlie Chaplin), and used similar protective and economic methods to attract its membership. It eventually became so strong, Popkin wrote, that landlords too began to join for their own protection against the now united peasants (pp. 193–199). This interweaving of social, cultural, and political factors took Popkin's analysis well beyond basic economic assumptions about human behavior.

Popkin's discussion of the development of the Communist organization in Vietnam also went well beyond strict political economy. Contrary to Olson's (1968) claim that no one will join any organization unless personal benefits are received (otherwise they will "free ride"), Popkin suggested that Communism succeeded because at least some of its leaders "were not stimulated by any expectation of future selective payoff," thus emphasizing "how important internalized feelings of duty or ethic can be" (Popkin, 1979, p. 223; see p. 254 for his remarks on Olson). While the members of Japanese- or Chinese-sponsored movements at the same period in Vietnamese history "worried about personal power, cabinet seats, and portfolios in a joint government of all parties, the Communists developed meaningful and exciting activities for those eager to secure the future" (p. 222).

In his conclusion, Popkin indicated that his theory involved modification of both the moral economy and the political economy approaches to develop a "political" model of his own.

> *In developing my approach, I have modified two views of peasant society. A free-market economics approach, even when amended to take account of*

peasant aversion to risk, cannot explain the patterns of stratification and production . . . in Vietnam without considering collective goods and leadership, political coalitions that shape markets, and the infrastructure of the economic system. . . . The moral economy approach . . . requires modification as well to take account of the ways in which aversion to risk, conflicts between public and private forms of investment, and conflicts among the peasantry limit the quality and extent of insurance and welfare embedded in peasant institutions. . . . (Popkin, 1979, p. 267).

Popkin's overall claim against the moral economists was that same position taken earlier by Marx in respect to English colonialism in India: that if colonialism was harsh, it was often less harsh than life under the village regime; and that if markets and capitalist economics destroyed a traditional way of life, they also provided opportunities for men to improve their economic conditions. Yet his argument was not incompatible with that of the moral economists but rather complementary, as when Popkin said that peasants would turn to wider marketplaces when they were "secure enough to want to raise their economic level and 'redefine' cultural standards" (Popkin, 1979, p. 80). Scott, of course, was not dealing primarily with secure peasants but with "drowning" ones. The Scott-Popkin controversy is educational but should not be overworked; in fact, each deals with the same kinds of actors, but actors who are forced to, or able to, respond in different ways to differing environmental conditions.[3]

FROM PEASANTS TO STATES AND SOCIETIES

The interest in grassroots political behavior out in peasant villages and the rural countryside was the origin of a new approach that enlarged upon the early studies in order to provide an alternative both to the state-centered framework and the older society-based functional approach. This new approach, called variously the state-society approach, or the state-and-society approach, or the state-in-society model, was misnamed insofar as it seemed to imply a sort of amalgamation of the earlier whole-system approaches; when in fact it was novel, within comparative politics at least, in its microanalytic method, its concern with actual individuals caught in their webs of state and society interactions. This was not a "bringing people back in," because the behavioralists had already tried that angle. Instead, it brought a particular new viewpoint on people back into focus, and might with some accuracy have been called "bringing politics back in." Not only were peasants enmeshed in relations with landlords, local leaders and miscellaneous outside functionaries, with all actions closely tied to crops, markets, and other physical circumstances; in addition, everyone, including state officials, came under the microscope as individuals pursuing their own goals in the face of their own political constraints.

Joel Migdal's *Strong Societies and Weak States* (1988) was the first full expression of this viewpoint, which has since become a school with its own theoretic assumptions and approaches, often defining itself against the earlier emphasis on the state as a unified, presumably autonomous actor (Migdal, Kohli, and Shue 1994). Students of comparative politics will find Migdal's contribution to the analysis of the field of comparative politics in the widely regarded survey of the political science discipline (Finifter, 1983), which meant that his theoretic efforts were grounded in a deep familiarity with the literature of the discipline, and were designed to respond to issues and questions raised by that literature.

Migdal introduced his 1988 book by calling attention to two important facts of political life in various parts of the world: first, the incredible changes in the political landscapes of even the most remote villages, but changes that were not what anyone seemed to have intended; and second, the way in which many leaders consciously and deliberately undercut the activities of their own state agencies, agencies that were supposed to be the leader's own instruments.

Migdal's familiarity with the wide range of theoretic approaches within comparative politics led him to a series of rejections that indicate both where the discipline has traveled in recent decades, and what had been left behind. The teleology of modernization theory—the idea that there is some kind of inevitability to the process of development—was the first to be discarded by Migdal; after it went the exclusive concern with the center's effect on the periphery, the emphasis on class as a decisive factor, the belief that revolutions determined social outcomes. Finally and methodologically, Migdal rejected both self-conscious theoretical efforts and the illusions of empiricists who think they can proceed without any theory at all.

This led to what he called an "integrated general essay" offering a state-society model that attempted to bring into better balance the various insights of past schools, emphasizing the distribution of social control among many organizations in society and government, toward answering the question of why third world states have such difficulty in becoming the predominant group in their society. It was a mark of Migdal's neutrality that he took no predetermined stand on which side of the battle—state or society—should win. Both states and societies exploit their members, he said, and it was not easy to choose which kind of exploitation is preferable (Migdal, 1988, p. xxi).

STRATEGIES OF SURVIVAL

The thread unifying our discussion of the various approaches adopted, utilized, and rejected by students of comparative politics in the search for a conceptual framework adequate to the empirically verifiable explanation of political phenomena in many nations, has been the need for and the sometimes desperate difficulty of finding concepts that worked, that organized data, that laid the basis for explanation, that helped make sense of the world. The approaches discussed here so far have largely tried to meet this need with the use of very large abstractions—stability, democracy, adaptation, integration, modernization, autonomy, and so on.

In contrast, Migdal's approach was microanalytic, focusing on political individuals and their dynamic political interactions, not on overarching summary abstractions. Rational choice theorists have been the only other school to have adopted microanalycity so thoroughly, but their "economic man" was himself abstracted from most contextual factors and so no real forerunner to Migdal's model. Because Migdal was interested both in the political periphery, which he felt had not been sufficiently studied, and in the core, where he admitted that most of the exciting events occur, Migdal needed a theoretical concept that would be applicable in both places, and found it in the notion of "strategies of survival" that are used by peasants, landlords, kings, presidents, and indeed everyone else who participates in the political and social worlds.

The strategies of survival concept highlights two factors essential to Migdal's purposes. First, the belief (or axiom) that all persons, high or low, enter onto their social or political careers in a highly specific context, a physical and institutional environment that they do not themselves create but that they inherit from the past. Such an environment is not set in cement—it can be changed—but it forms a starting position, and establishes the "problem" with which the individual actor must deal. A man may be born the son of a cacique, or of a landless peasant; where he starts is absolutely decisive in respect to where he can get to, and how. In addition to the importance of the environment, Migdal emphasized the active problem-solving activities of the individuals who were the actors in political events, actors who had intellects, goals, personal ambitions, social and political resources they used in building strategies of survival.

Taking these analytic perspectives into the issue of state building in the Third World, Migdal asked under what conditions states become strong, studying specifically Egypt, India, Israel, Mexico, and Sierra Leone. His question, stated in a different way, was why leaders' policies met resistance and why leaders could or could not overcome this resistance (Migdal, 1988, p. 9). Here Migdal painted a picture not of an absolute state facing a unified society, but instead a *melange* of organizations adjacent, competing, embedded, all influencing individuals; organizations that defined what people could do, or think, or hope for; organizations that could bestow a livelihood or take it away, could assist or impede survival.

These organizations and individuals provided persons not just with incentives but with packages of incentives, incentives tied together into bundles of both good and bad things by the persons who sought control: you may have this or that good, but in return you must give up your rights to this or that option or resource (Migdal, 1988, pp. 24–26). Migdal saw society as the various groups and individuals linked by these mutual incentive bundles, so that there might be a lot of authority in a system but fragmented authority; the state is only one organization among many, or more accurately one cluster of organizations among many other clusters (pp. 28–29). Political life here is not the World Series, giant against giant, but a vast spread of ballparks where "many ballgames may be played simultaneously" (p. 39).

The survival viewpoint contained as an important theoretic feature an emphasis on the connection between material political struggles and "moral economies." Distinguishing moral economies from "rational" action, Migdal said, missed the dynamic nature of their interaction: People "combine available symbols with opportunities" in service of their needs, to create "blueprints for action and belief in a world that hovers on the brink of a Hobbesian state of nature" (Migdal, 1988, p. 27). The choice of a person's or a leader's strategies was constrained by available ideas and organizations; the political struggle held at its core the question of who would be allowed control over the rules that govern assets and resources (p. 28).

WHY SOCIETIES FAIL

In regard to state building, Migdal's central contention was that states' capacity or incapacity depends on the "environment of conflict" in the society (Migdal, 1988, p. 34). Strong states are few; he listed Israel, Cuba, China, Japan, Vietnam, Taiwan, the Koreas. The conditions that lead to strong states are large and perhaps idiosyncratic: (1) massive societal dislocation, weakening societies sufficiently to make new forms of control possible; (2) mass migration that disrupts existing social patterns and makes room for the state; (3) world historical moments such as colonialism or the Cold War; (4) outside military threats that force leaders to confront local strongmen; (5) a skilled national bureaucracy; and (6) skilled leadership (pp. 270–275).

The hazards of leadership, and an example of survival politics for elite actors, were illustrated by Egypt's agrarian reform. As Migdal analyzed the episode, Nasser succeeded in breaking the biggest landlords but had underestimated their role in maintaining local stability, and had no agencies ready to replace them. While Nasser might have used his political party to replace local control, that party had itself become a threat to his own power in the absence of countervailing power centers in the country. He therefore had to undercut his own policies in order to save his political skin (pp. 183–205).

In many cases the national political struggle leads not to reform and progress but to what Migdal calls triangles of accommodations, where middle level officials ("implementors") engage in a panoply of well-known bureaucratic maneuvers to maintain their survival in the face of often conflicting demands upon them by their supervisors, their clients, local leaders, and bureaucratic peers. Accommodations between leaders and strongmen, and regionally between implementors and strongmen, create policy webs that then define survival strategies for the public (Migdal, 1988, pp. 238–247). This is why, to return to Migdal's initial question, states so widely influence societies, but not in the manner anyone intended.

While Migdal presented *Strong Societies and Weak States* as an "essay" without theoretical preconceptions or pretensions, it is important not to be led astray by this reticence into failing to notice how extensive is the conceptual originality of the work. Since comparative politics determined decades ago to reject the traditional past and chart a new dynamic future for itself, there has been a good deal of activity best characterized as thrashing the bushes in the hope a usable idea would fly forth. In general, this has not happened. Students of comparative politics have borrowed ideas from others, have reified their own Western preferences, have sided with the wretched of the earth, have gone down many roads all the way to numerous dead ends, all in the search for "universal" theories. The theories failed because they were so universal they were inapplicable to any actual situation, thus considerably diminishing their ability to guide research.

The state-society, or the *melange*, model presented by Migdal solves several grand problems with extreme neatness. First, the model is concrete, centered upon individuals and their behavior, and is therefore easy to apply. Second, while the state-society model reduces political phenomena to the behavior of individuals, it is not reductionist in the justly criticized sense of removing from those individuals all the special characteristics that make them real; instead, it includes those characteristics— resources, official position, purposes, skills. Third and relatedly, by enmeshing individuals in socioeconomic and political interrelationships and institutions, the model provides for those enduring structural features that are so important in political analysis, while also showing how individual behaviors serve to maintain, create, or destroy these institutions as the result of political activity. Finally and not least important, the model seems everywhere applicable; as comparativists used to say, "it will travel" to any situation involving political individuals interacting with one another, and with outcomes depending on strategies, circumstances, and environmental parameters— from peasant villages to 10 Downing Street, from legislatures to landlords, from the highest politics to the lowest.

An exemplary case of the wide usefulness of such embedded models comes from another "nontheorist," the African specialist J. Gus Liebenow, who sought to explain the prevalence of military governments on the African continent by showing them as the unintended results of elite interaction in colonial and post-colonial governments. The interactive model here included not only a melange of groups struggling for survival in circumstances that they did not choose, but the role of specific beliefs and expectations on the parts of participants, and the way in which the strategic interactions themselves create and change the players.

AFRICAN ELITE POLITICS AND THE MILITARY

Looking first at the position of African elites under colonialism, Liebenow selected two features as particularly significant in their political "education" by events: First, the elites underestimated the colonial governments; second, the elites overestimated themselves. The elites' underestimation of colonial governments resulted, according to Liebenow, in part from the skills of the European administrators, who had generations of bureaucratic experience to draw upon and were able because of the situation to be efficient, ruthlessly efficient if necessary. African elites therefore tended, Liebenow argued, to think that governing was easy (Liebenow, 1986, pp. 242–244). Their perception of colonial governments as illegitimate led the elites further to suppose that when colonial rule was abolished there would be much less need for the use of force, because indigenous government would have legitimacy and could rule gently.

Along with this underestimation of the problems of governing; Liebenow said, elites overestimated their own capacities, based on years of experience when the primary skills needed by political party leaders were rhetorical, mobilizing the public through charismatic appeals rather than policy proposals (Liebenow, 1986, pp. 240–241). Under colonial conditions, in fact, a rousing speech needed to do very little more than document the latest outrage committed by the Europeans and was guaranteed an enthusiastic response (p. 231).

Given these two misperceptions, when the colonial administrators left and the indigenous elites took over government functions, they believed they would not need much help from the military and gave it few of their scarce resources. In many cases, Liebenow argued, the military forces were recruited from the least modernized regions, were seen as useful only for ceremonial occasions, and were not given much education; but in fact military life itself was a modernizing factor, introducing its members to the cash economy, health and sanitation, vehicles and machines. This made it a desirable career alternative (Liebenow, 1986, pp. 246–247).

When government proved more troublesome than expected (the colonial rulers had done more conflict mediation among competing indigenous groups than they had been given credit for), the new elites turned to the military to maintain their shaky rule, using force against secessionists, student demonstrators, and striking laborers. But by undercutting the strength of the military, then using it to cover the government's own failures to maintain order, the government created resentment in the military against the civilian authorities, and began to create a "military monster," he argued.

RELATED STRATEGIES

The next mistake Liebenow defined was that the leaders belatedly began to fear the military and worse, began to show their fear; they cut military budgets, which was a direct challenge to the military's self-interest in salaries, uniforms, and housing; and civilians also began to interfere with promotions, thus threatening the military's authority over its own structure. Finally, admitting the degree of their fear, the civilian elites established special paramilitary forces to protect themselves, or failing all else hired foreign troops. Others tried to bribe high military officials, thereby increasing their contempt, and their tendency to coup (Liebenow, 1986, pp. 247–249).

After the military takeover, according to Liebenow's account, the dynamic process of learning and change continued. Upon taking power the first thing the military learned was that it had overestimated the depth of its popular support; its legitimacy declined because its mandate was to restore civilian rule, and the longer it failed to do this the worse things became. As lofty aims gave way to narrow corporate self-interest, the military found that it had to rely on technicians it could not adequately control, and it was unable by its very structure to make the compromises necessary for governing. Internal power conflicts also beset the military, where the troops were of different ethnic background from the top brass, or interservice rivalries over power and perquisites brought internal divisions (Liebenow, 1986, pp. 253–255). The military's claim to maintain social order therefore collapsed into government by disappearance and death squad (p. 261).

Liebenow's model of the process by which militaries come to dominate is particularly revealing in its dynamism. African militaries were not in his view inherent dangers to political rule, but became dangerous as a result of a particular historical experience. By understanding events at this microanalytic level, such models are open to the possibility of varying some elements and perhaps avoiding some of the undesirable outcomes.

The patterns Liebenow described in this model will hold only under certain circumstances, but his method is becoming more and more typical of comparative research. By focusing on the political and institutional interaction of concrete individuals, peculiarities of forms of government or economies or regions of the world are stripped away and only the core model remains: leaders and peoples and groups, enmeshed in their own mutual struggles for survival and control and precedence, within rules and institutions that they inherit but may remake continually as the political game continues through their history.

THE NEW INSTITUTIONALISM IN POLITICAL ANALYSIS

The movement known in political science as the new institutionalism appears to travel under a clear brand name that should assure the user of product consistency, but closer analysis shows such wide differences in the approaches of its various adherents that the term becomes more a flag of convenience than a meaningful label. The locus classicus of the new institutionalism, the publication that first set forth the array of ideas that came to be known by the name, was a 1984 article in the prestigious *American Political Science Review* by two well-known authors, James March and Johan Olsen. Titled "The New Institutionalism: Organizational Factors in Political Life," the article was essentially an attack on the behavioral movement, although the authors did not use that term but referred instead to "theories of politics since 1950," or "modern political theory," or "contemporary theories of politics." Such theories placed less emphasis, according to March and Olsen, on traditional political institutions such as legislatures, legal systems, and the state; less emphasis on traditional economic institutions such as the firm; and reduced institutions simply to "arenas within which political behavior, driven by more fundamental factors, occurs."

Older views in which citizenship was seen as the basis of personal identity and in which morality was grounded in institutions such as law and bureaucracy had been replaced, in the behavioral view of politics, by moral individualism and the definition of politics as the struggle over conflicts of interest, March and Olsen argued. The new institutionalism, they said, involved students of legislatures, budgets, public policy, local government, political elites, state and national development, corporatism, neo-statism, organizations, policy implementation; all of whom shared a belief in the power and complexity of institutional factors in political life.

March and Olsen compared and contrasted the behavioral approach with their new institutionalist alternative along five specific dimensions that highlighted differences at the most fundamental levels. While it is possible to claim the authors not only clarified but exaggerated the differences, the exercise is valuable in providing the grandest possible overview of the discipline and the ongoing controversy over paradigms.

The first difference March and Olsen defined was between "modern political scientists" who explained political events as arising from contextual factors such as social class, economics, religion, and other similar factors, with no reciprocal effect by politics on these conditions; and the institutionalists who saw the state and other political institutions as independent factors in shaping collective life. March and Olsen's second difference between behavioralists and institutionalists was that behavioralists reduced all explanations to the individual or group level of social and economic influences, and assumed that collective groups were simply the aggregate of individual actions, as in the theory of markets; while the institutionalists saw institutions as having a real influence upon individual behavior.

The third difference between the schools was that behavioralists used rational choice models involving individual calculations of utility, and ignored the impact of institutional rules, routines, and norms, on individual behavior. The fourth was that behavioralists assumed the individual choice model led to progress and efficient historical processes and quite ignored negative results. Finally, March and Olsen contrasted the two approaches in the area of ideas: for behavioralists, they said, symbols and rituals were defined as false and manipulative, used by politicians who said one thing and did another; while for institutionalists, politics created identity and a sense of purpose, and educated its citizens in cultural values (March and Olsen, 1984, pp. 736–738).[4]

INSTITUTIONS AS CAUSES

March and Olsen did not argue for a return to the old institutionalism, even in the idealized version they described, which rather overlooked the predominant amount of time the old institutionalists spent in sterile institutional description of ethnocentrically evaluated political structures. Rather the authors called for a blending of the old and new, emphasizing the relative autonomy of state and society, and the role of rich historical processes in forming outcomes. They placed special emphasis on the design of institutions—agencies, committees, and courts are not just "arenas" where individuals struggle, but are influential structures "that define and defend interests"

(March and Olsen, 1984, p. 739). Where behavioralists saw individual preferences as stable, and resources as fixed, March and Olsen described a new institutionalist approach in which the political process and political experience changed and developed both preferences and resources. Choices are not clearly defined, as decision theorists suppose, March and Olsen said, but must be searched out in a complex environment that includes institutional opportunities and constraints (p. 740).

The new institutionalist alternative, as described by March and Olsen, defined not an arena of decision makers acting in freedom and clarity but a more solid world where institutions, rules, norms, roles, and physical arrangements were "relatively invariant in the face of turnover of individuals." Rather than individuals subject only to personal preferences and expectations, March and Olsen saw duties and obligations as controlling action, and defined a "duty metaphor" according to which "actions associate certain actions with certain situations by rules of appropriateness" defined by the system. The rule-driven hypothesis should direct investigation toward an examination of how history "is encoded into rules," and what effect this encoding has upon future outcomes (March and Olsen, 1984, p. 741).

Here, however, March and Olsen's argument slightly shifted its ground, moving from the almost unarguable empirical thesis that institutions are important factors in political life, to a quite speculative thesis that institutions are morally good. The new institutionalism, March and Olsen argued, was based on the ancient theme of political thought that in politics "individuals develop themselves, their communities, and the public good. . . . participation in civic life is the highest form of activity for a civilized person." "Politics is regarded as education, as a place for discovering, elaborating, and expressing meanings, establishing shared (or opposing) conceptions of experience, values, and the nature of existence" (March and Olsen, 1984, p. 741).

Evidence for the moral trend in the new institutionalism is provided by many recruits to the school, who are openly or implicitly attracted by the possibility it contains that institutions can serve to better human life by helping it to escape normlessness and conflict.[5] Yet insofar as apartheid, national socialism, terrorism, and state-sponsored death squads all qualify as institutions, one must suggest that the belief in the beneficence of all institutions somewhat strains credulity, and weakens the argument for the approach.

"HISTORICAL" INSTITUTIONALISM

The breadth of the differences among new institutionalists in political science was illustrated by a recent collection of articles representing the new institutionalism in its historical, sociological, and qualitative variant (Steinmo, Thelen, and Longstreth, 1992), as distinguished from the rational choice variety. In their analytic introduction to this book, Thelen and Steinmo reemphasized the new institutionalists' defining controversy with the behavioralists, who "often obscured the enduring socioeconomic and political structures that mold behavior in distinctive ways in different national contexts" (Thelen and Steinmo, 1992, p. 1). Attempting to synthesize a literature that is highly diverse, even within the subschool of historical institutionalism, Thelen and Steinmo noted the general agreement in both schools on the importance of institutions in mediating political struggles, and the new institutionalists' willingness to include "both formal organizations and informal rules and procedures that structure conflict" (Thelen and Steinmo, 1992, p. 2).

Because historical institutionalism is difficult to define in terms of any specific model, the authors chose to define it by its contrasts with the rational choice version: Both shared "a concern with the question of how institutions shape political strategies and influence political outcomes," but each was "premised on different assumptions that in fact reflect quite different approaches to the study of politics" (Thelen and Steinmo 1992, p. 7). The first difference they listed was the difference in scope. Where rational choice theorists are concerned with the ways in which institutions influence standard choice situations, such as the Prisoner's Dilemma, by constraining self-interested behavior, historical institutionalists "want to go further and argue that institutions play a much greater role in shaping politics and political history."

REASON AND DUTY

The issue of rationality as a theoretic concept is of central importance among new institutionalists, but advocates of the various positions in the debate do not necessarily agree in their approach to rational decision models: Some writers on both sides want to maintain rational norms intact, and some on both sides seek to widen the behavioral rules relevant to choice. Historical institutionalists generally believe that people tend to "follow societally defined rules" even when it is not in their self-interest, according to Thelen and Steinmo. Among rational choice theorists, however, there is vigorous advocacy both for and against a strong rationality assumption.

Related to the issue of rationality in choice is the question of where preferences come from, or, in other words, how self-interest is defined. Where new institutionalists from the rational choice school usually adopt a static set of preferences, deductively defined as selfish maximization, historical new institutionalists want to argue that the institutions within which people find themselves have a major role in determining what their preferences will be, as well as their strategies; Steinmo and Thelen here referred as an illustration to Thorstein Veblen who maintained that individualism and competitiveness in society are not innate but socially engrained (Thelen and Steinmo, 1992, p. 8).

Another major difference in the two new institutionalist variants, indeed perhaps the major difference, is in methodology, the authors said. Readers of works in the rational choice variant of the new institutionalism will often be hard pressed to separate it from the long-running "behavioral" mode of political economy going back to Downs, Olson, and Riker. The tools used by both are purely economic: deductive analysis of what idealized economic people will "rationally" do in strategic interaction situations where behavior is based on a very narrow range of individual goals, usually just monetary profit. Such theory aims to be universal, applicable to all societies under all conditions, and claims that the slightest relaxation of its parameters will vitiate its scientific quality. Historical institutionalists, on the other hand, work inductively, or as their critics complain, "tell stories" about how particular events occurred in particular conditions (Steinmo et al., 1992, p. 12).

Not only is there no deductively rigorous theory in historical institutionalism, there often seems no theory at all, claims about "middle range" theorizing to the contrary. In the particular area that historical institutionalists designate as their special province—institutional change—theory fails because institutions themselves have not been rigorously specified in the kind of empirical form that would allow change to be actually described. In part this follows from the habit, illustrated by the contributors to the collection, of analyzing whole-nation policy phenomena. The excessive size of nation-states and the complexity of identifying all the relevant variables in, say, working class formation in England, or railroad policy in the United States and Prussia, precludes the kind of close analysis upon which middle-range theory might be built.[6]

THE RATIONAL CHOICE VARIANT IN THE NEW INSTITUTIONALISM

An example of some of the research characteristic of rational choice analysis among neoinstitutionalists is a recent work by Elinor Ostrom, a political scientist who has given greater attention than have most to the development of theory to support new institutionalist research concerns. The study, titled *Governing the Commons: The Evolution of Institutions for Collective Action* (Ostrom, 1990), took its starting point from a classic dilemma in rational choice theory, Russell Hardin's "tragedy of the commons," which along with the Prisoner's Dilemma has given theorists endless trouble insofar as it indicates that when individuals act rationally the result is social irrationality. Hardin's tragedy is simple: In a small community where people can use the common land for grazing their animals, it will be individually rational for each villager to increase the number of his or her livestock using the common land—but if everyone does this, the common will be overgrazed and the collective good will be destroyed. The problem has obvious relevance in the modern world where the environment is under constant and dangerous stress from overuse, and in which irrecoverable resources are constantly lost.

Ostrom's study of governing common resources focused directly on this problem of natural resource destruction, working from the assumption that neither market solutions nor the state have successfully solved the need for sustainable development, but sometimes small groups of individuals have themselves done it. Like many new institutionalist works, the Ostrom book was labelled by the series editors as "positive rather than normative" in content (Alt and North in Ostrom, p. xi), but the book nonetheless showed strong commitment to the optimistic belief that institutions can serve a positive function in solving collective action problems.

Ostrom's approach took a middle course here, studying both successful and failed cases, using a remarkably broad database, including communal mountain and forest tenure in Switzerland; common lanes in Japan; Spanish and Philippine irrigation systems; water problems in California; and Turkish, Sri Lankan, and Nova Scotian fisheries.

The problem situation in each case was the management of a "common pool resource," and Ostrom separated her approach from many others in political science by assuming neither that individuals are omnisciently rational nor entirely "incompetent, evil, or irrational." She studied policy issues in relatively small-scale situations, she said, in order better "to penetrate the surface complexity to identify underlying similarities and processes"; but the cases chosen are in a relatively narrow area of collective action—renewable resources where participants' positions are relatively symmetrical (Ostrom, 1990, p. 26). "Governing the commons" was heavily indebted to classic rational choice theory and game theory, and refers back constantly not only to Hardin's tragedy and the Prisoner's Dilemma, but also of Mancur Olson's model of free riders as an intractable barrier to collective action (1968).

WHO ORGANIZES WHAT, HOW?

The central question defined by Ostrom was "how a group of principals who are in an interdependent situation can organize and govern themselves to obtain continuing joint benefits when all face temptations to free-ride, shirk, or otherwise act opportunistically" (Ostrom, 1990, p. 29). Two accepted theories exist about how to avoid "the adverse outcomes of independent action"—the theory of the state and the theory of the firm—but little work has been attempted on self-organization. Ostrom defined three specific questions: (1) Why are institutions created, (2) once institutions exist why does not everyone cheat, and (3) how can participants monitor compliance? In rational choice theory's world of self-interested maximizers, institutions constitute a pure dilemma: Without monitoring there will be no credible commitments; without credible commitments there is no reason to propose new rules. "The process unravels from both ends" and the mystery is how it ever succeeds, as empirical observation tells us it sometimes does succeed" (Ostrom, 1990, p. 45).[7]

In making her analyses, Ostrom described her approach as follows:

> . . . I first try to understand something about the structure of the resource itself—its size, clarity of boundary, and internal structure. Then I try to discover the flow patterns involved in the resource units: How much predictability is involved over time, across space, and in quantity? Given the economic circumstances of the appropriators, how reliant are they on the resource, and what are the risks involved in various potential types of alloca-

tion schemes? Lastly I try to ascertain key attributes of the individuals: How many are involved? What are their time horizons likely to be? Are they involved in multiple activities together? Are their interests roughly similar or heterogeneous? Have they established prior norms of behavior that can be drawn on (or pose a disadvantage) in trying to solve these problems? Then I examine the rules that they have devised and try to understand how they work by searching for the design principles that are involved and how these affect the incentives of participants. Given that the appropriators in these cases have engaged in mutual monitoring and generally have kept their commitments to follow their rules to a substantial degree, I try to understand how they have been able to do this (p. 56).

Ostrom combined a "very broad" definition of rationality, including the individual's internal norms (Ostrom, 1990, p. 37), along with a heavy reliance on the structure of the specific situation and an artful use by participants of nested rules, as ways of explaining policy outcomes (pp. 46, 50). Institutions were defined "as the sets of working rules that are used to determine who is eligible to make decisions in some arena, what actions are allowed or constrained, what aggregation rules will be used, what procedures must be followed, what information must or must not be provided, and what payoffs will be assigned to individuals dependent on their actions." Ostrom especially emphasized the various levels of rules that affect individual action, and the consensuality of the rules. Where working rules forbid, permit, or require some specific action or outcome, deeper constraints involve the rules of collective choice and are harder to change (pp. 51–54).

INSTITUTIONAL DESIGN PRINCIPLES

Using a series of cases that began in "the mists of time," Ostrom suggested certain principles that appeared to work towards success in creating institutions, including group autonomy, clear social boundaries, widespread participation, active monitoring, graduated enforcement sanctions, and efficient conflict resolution (Ostrom, 1990, p. 90). These circumstances she contrasted with the usual rational choice assumptions of large-scale societies, no communication, independent action, indifference to the whole, and the difficulty of changing institutional structure; and she argued that the Prisoner's Dilemma and similar models are not so much wrong as not universally appropriate (p. 183).

Ostrom's conclusion included an "institutional choice" model showing an individual with two basic alternatives, to support or maintain the rules currently in existence, or to support a change in some or all of these rules (Ostrom, 1990, p. 193). The model involves difficult calculations in any effort to estimate the costs and benefits of the various alternatives, however, and requires that the individuals "behave in a straightforward, rather than a strategic manner" to simplify the analysis to the point where it becomes possible to achieve (p. 194). This utter disregard of "politics" is one of the weakest aspects of new institutionalist theory.

THE INSTITUTIONAL MODEL

Because the discussion among new institutionalists, state-society theorists, and other analytic institutionalist scholars is still raging, it would be premature to make any definitive formulation that might seem to prejudge future developments. Yet certain basic dimensions of the individual-in-institutions model are clear.

1. First of all, the model generally defines individual actors as having many goals; a situation that comparative politics students have always understood because of their rich experience with many different types of societies. The assumptions of rational choice theory are slowly but surely failing to prevail in emphasizing only monetary utility, when the world is full of people with many goals, from the social, to the political, to the cultural, and to the spiritual.

2. Second, the approach agrees that institutions are created by human beings and cannot be understood in isolation from the history of their creation, which is full of purposes and mistakes, of deliberate intentions, and of unforseen consequences. Institutions are neither timeless nor absolute, and have no existence beyond the people who believe and enforce them.

3. Third and equally important, however, is the controlling effect of existing institutions, which by their mere presence when people are born into a given society take on an appearance of timeless immutability. Virtually every human act is conditioned by institutions, which provide rules for everything from personal habits to the meaning of life.

4. The analytic institutional model takes on life from its premise of political actors as "political," as pursuing survival within institutional constraints with all the political means at their disposal, including changing, bending, or eluding the institutions. This covers a lot of ground, from peasants to heads of state, and since such behavior occurs in every society, this model provides a good basis for systematic comparative inquiry.

5. Finally, the analytic institutionalism model emphasizes a methodological approach that is concerned less with the statistical correlations typical of behavioralism and more than statist approaches with scientific rigor. These attitudes are reflected in the model as a search for explanatory depth, and the approach can often be recognized by the amount of circumstantial detail in its accounts, and its strong attention to the underlying logic of the participants' behavior (Lane, 1990).

The simplest and most appropriate name for this new approach might be the politics model, to distinguish it from economic, social, and psychological models of the past by its emphasis on persons as the creatures of, and creators of, the institutions within which they live, using every political means, both high and low, at their disposal.

NOTES

1. The well-known Prisoner's Dilemma game involves two suspects who are separated by the sheriff and urged to confess to a crime; the issue is what each is to do, not knowing what the other will do. If both confess, each gets eight years; if both keep silence, each gets one year; but if one squeals, he is let off with a token sentence of three months while the other has the book thrown at him, that is, a ten-year term in the slammer. The problem is that while both would benefit by keeping quiet, the payoff matrix requires "rational" players to confess (to avoid being made the sucker), and this outcome is worse than they would have by cooperating (see Luce and Raiffa, 1957, pp. 94–97). Scott's peasants have in effect made a prior agreement to cooperate, thereby avoiding the worst outcome.

2. In the same footnote Popkin remarks that in some cases the poor are given rights to gather the peas of others (Popkin, 1979, note 64, p. 67). This is one among the many passing admissions in the book that the moral economy does exist, in parallel with the political economy.

3. Booth (1993) has pointed out that the controversy between the moral and the political economists is false, in the sense that the claim of the moral economists about collective village norms is "entirely consistent with the economic approach to human behavior," because they employ "an economic explanation of the dominance of nonmarket institutions," and that if the scarcity constraints are relaxed then the "moral" peasants will act like "economic" peasants (pp. 950–951).

4. It should be noted that March himself had a major role in advancing the behavioral approach; see, for instance, Lave and March (1975).

5. See, for instance, Levi (1988), Ostrom (1990).

6. The close political analysis used by Skowronek (1982) in his studies of the U.S. civil service and military organization is a good example of how detailed analysis can be achieved, even where the national political stage is at issue.

7. It is grievous that new institutionalists so rarely read traditional political theory. Rousseau had a classic answer here. It is found in his "Discourse on Inequality" and has rarely been surpassed.

REFERENCES

Booth, William James. "A Note on the Idea of the Moral Economy." *American Political Science Review* 87, no. 4 (December 1993): 949–54.

Finifter, Ada W. *The State of Discipline II.* Washington: American Political Science Association, 1993.

Hardin, Garrett. "The Tragedy of the Commons." *Science* 162 (13 December 1968): 1243–48.

Lane, Ruth. "Concrete Theory: An Emerging Political Method." *American Political Science Review* 84, no. 3 (September 1990): 927–40.

Lave, Charles A., and James G. March. *An Introduction to Models in the Social Sciences*. New York: Harper and Row, 1975.

Levi, Margaret. *Of Rule's Revenue*. Berkeley: University of California Press, 1988.

Liebenow, J. Gus. *African Politics: Crises and Challenges*. Bloomington: Indiana University Press, 1986.

Luce, R. Duncan, and Howard Raiffa. *Games and Decisions: Introduction and Critical Survey*. New York: Wiley, 1957.

March, James G., and Johan P. Olsen. "The New Institutionalism: Organizational Factors in Political Life." *American Political Science Review* LXXVIII (1984): 734–49.

March, James G., and Johan P. Olsen. *Rediscovering Institutions: The Organizational Basis of Politics*. New York: The Free Press, 1989.

Migdal, Joel S. *Strong Societies and Weak States: State-Society Relations and State Capabilities in the Third World*. Princeton: Princeton University Press, 1988.

Migdal, Joel S., Atul Kohli, and Vivienne Shue. *State Power and Social Forces*. Cambridge: Cambridge University Press, 1994.

Olson, Mancur, Jr. *The Logic of Collective Action*. New York: Schocken, 1968.

Ostrom, Elinor. *Governing the Commons: The Evolution of Institutions for Collective Action*. Cambridge: Cambridge University Press, 1990.

Popkin, Samuel L. *The Rational Peasant: The Political Economy of Rural Society in Vietnam*. Berkeley: University of California Press, 1979.

Scott, James C. *The Moral Economy of the Peasant: Rebellion and Subsistence in Southeast Asia*. New Haven: Yale University Press, 1976.

Skowronek, Stephen. *Building a New American State*. New York: Cambridge University Press, 1982.

Steinmo, Sven, Kathleen Thelen, and Frank Longstreth (Eds.). *Structuring Politics: Historical Institutionalism in Comparative Analysis*. Cambridge: Cambridge University Press, 1992.

Thelen, Kathleen, and Sven Steinmo. "Historical Institutionalism in Comparative Politics." In Sven Steinmo, Kathleen Thelen, and Frank Longstreth (Eds.), *Structuring Politics: Historical Institutionalism in Comparative Analysis* (pp. 1–32). Cambridge: Cambridge University Press, 1992.

► 6

Theory and the Art of Comparative Politics

What is a theory? Observers of comparative politics, whether they have been engaged in the field for a very long or a very short time period, may all equally find themselves asking this question. Most writers on the subject of research theory tend to take a critical position that is one-dimensional; there is a scale along which different types of theory can be ranged, and the writer's own favorite theory stands at the top of this scale, casting all others into the implacable shadows of paradigmatic imperfection. Such a one-dimensional view of theory is both egocentric and excessively dogmatic for a discipline such as political science that is so early in its scientific journey.[1]

By way of shedding light on the question, What is theory?, two strategies suggest themselves. First is the analysis of three contemporary forms of theory that have both historical and intellectual claims upon the attention of comparativists. Along with discussing both strong and weak points of the three theories, it is especially important to show how each theory can be appreciated for itself, and how each can be utilized for future research by being enlarged, or applied, or (sometimes) by being thrown out entirely except for one or two crucial lessons.

A second approach to theory is the study of model building in general, an exercise for which it is appropriate to recall a classic work by Charles Lave and James March (1975), which shows how theories are constructed and how such a do-it-yourself strategy can put social scientists on the cutting edges of their fields. It is also an approach that is directly parallel to the kind of theory-building that has been the subject of the present work.

The exploration of the nature of theory begins first with some exemplary theories in political science. The first theory on the list is an old "prebehavioral" theory,

Michels' iron law of oligarchy; the second is a much more classically abstract theory, functionalism; the third is that much admired and much vilified school, rational choice theory. The basic principle underlying the discussion is that it is not useful to set up lists of what "good" theory should be, because lists by their nature tend to be disconnected, thin, sterile, and artificial. It is much more useful to study actual theories, to learn to evaluate these theories kindly and intelligently, and to use these theories as guides to intellectual analysis. And for these purposes, a picture of a real theory is worth a thousand definitions.

IRON-CLAD THEORY IN POLITICAL SCIENCE

Robert Michels' theory has a paradoxical position in American political science, because while virtually every member of the discipline is familiar with "the iron law of oligarchy," the substance of the theory is largely ignored. This is clearly a result of Michels' unpalatable conclusion; if, as the theory of oligarchy holds, small elites invariably control social groups, then democracy is impossible. Michels' own response to this problem is both cheerful and unsatisfying. He offers the story of an old peasant who, on his deathbed, tells his sons there is a fortune buried in the fields, but fails to tell them exactly where. The sons therefore vigorously dig up the land for years, vastly improving the soil quality, the harvests, and their wealth; but never finding the supposedly buried goal. Democracy is like this ephemeral gold, Michels says,

> *a treasure which no one will ever discover by deliberate search. But in continuing our search, in laboring indefatigably to discover the indiscoverable, we shall perform a work which will have fertile results in the democratic sense (Michels, 1959, p. 405).*

While economic development and the spread of education will increase the strength of democratic movements, Michels argues, in general the oligarchic struggles—the battles between different elites to control the people—constitute a cruel game, "that will continue without end" (Michels, 1959, pp. 406, 408). It is interesting here to recall one of the "behavioralist" works discussed earlier, Dahl's study of New Haven elites, since *Who Governs?* (1961) wholly supports the thesis of elite rule. Dahl, however, called it polyarchy, which put a better face on the matter without substantially changing the thrust of the argument.[2]

Many people feel that the very phrase, "the iron law of oligarchy," tells all one needs to know about Michels' theory, yet there is much more to be discovered in this classic example of "real theory" in the social sciences. Michels' book first of all represents a neat example of what is meant by the levels of theory, according to which a theory has a hierarchy of applications from the most specific to the most general. It is undoubtedly accurate to say, indeed, that a good theory must have this full array of levels—those that are only specific lack clout, those that are only general lack bite.

Michels' book encapsulates first a theory of European socialist parties, then a theory of similar ideological parties (including, for instance, syndicalists), then a theory of European parties generally (various conservative or catch-all parties) with an occasional reference to U.S. or Latin American parties; then rises to other working class organizations such as labor unions. At further higher levels of abstraction, Michels shows that his theory reaches not just parties but to the government as a whole, to the state itself; finally, at the highest and broadest analytic level, the theory applies to all organizations of whatever type—thus the "iron law".[3]

THE LAW OF OLIGARCHY

As a socialist of the old-fashioned warm-hearted kind, whose only goal is a true democracy in which all social classes equally share, Michels' often-repeated purpose in the analysis is to find out how democracy may be achieved and preserved. The text is therefore infused with his lack of neutrality, yet this bias does not diminish the clarity of his vision, as the behavioralists assumed such bias inevitably would do. Instead, his hopes for democracy increase the sharpness with which Michels faces the paradoxes his study reveals, as he inquires into the causal infrastructure that produces the government of human organizations.

The iron law of oligarchy, which Michels calls a "universally applicable social law," is finally stated in the conclusion of the book after having been implied, discussed, and illustrated for the previous almost 400 pages:

> . . . *every organ of the collectivity, brought into existence through the need for the division of labour, creates for itself as soon as it becomes consolidated, interests peculiar to itself. The existence of these special interests involves a necessary conflict with the interests of the collectivity (Michels, 1959, p. 389).*

Special attention should be directed to the word "every" in this statement, because it brings Michels' law into exact correspondence with the Popper-Hempel school of positivist thought, which required that any scientific law or hypothesis should be universally applicable. Very few social theories even attempt to meet such a stringent criterion; even natural scientists have some difficulty achieving it.[4]

Theories in political science, especially, are often so cluttered with qualifications that they make no claim to universality at all—and are therefore equivalent, as some critics have remarked balefully, to saying that water runs downhill except on Sundays and in Argentina. But Michels not only claims to present a universally applicable law, he makes a strongly documented case for its validity. Since his brief definition is perhaps unduly succinct to give the full flavor of the theory, it is useful to look at it in somewhat more detail.

THE CAUSAL MODEL

Michels bases his theory of oligarchy on two quite separate foundations, first, the technical side, involving the necessity of leadership in human affairs, and secondly, the psychological side, involving men's love of domination. The technical argument is based on the premise that the "sovereign masses are altogether incapable of undertaking the most necessary resolutions" (Michels, 1959, p. 25). This results in part from sheer numbers, but also on the masses' disinterest in anything but their own immediate affairs and their resulting ignorance of important issues. That this fact still holds even in modern educated societies is supported by works in the Olson school, which document the difficulty of interesting anyone in collective action; as well as by any public opinion poll, where citizens show themselves innocent of the most basic facts about politics and government policy.[5]

Because of the impossibility of direct democracy, Michels continues, it is necessary to delegate decision-making power to representatives who will carry out the will of the masses; and while initially all members of the mass are equal, certain talents are necessary for such delegates, and these skills differentiate them from nondelegates or nonleaders (Michels, 1959, pp. 27-28). "Organization implies the tendency to oligarchy," and as a result of organization "every party or professional union becomes divided into a minority of directors and a majority of directed," until "a rigorously defined and hierarchical bureaucracy" is created (pp. 32, 34). This leads Michels to the conclusion that mass voting, usually thought to be the mark of true democracy, is actually its opposite, for in the act of voting one renounces one's right to rule, one's sovereignty, by bestowing it on someone else, and representative government is a fraud, disguising the wills of the leaders as the will of the mass (pp. 38, 40).

Intimately joined with this view of the bitter fruits of organization is Michels' recognition of the even more bitter results of nonorganization, for he repeatedly refers to the incompetence of the masses, and is equally emphatic that "no undertaking can succeed without leaders, without managers," and their authority must necessarily increase for the good of the whole (Michels, 1959, p. 89). Leaders therefore must have oratorical skills, suppleness of mind, physical presence, force of will, breadth of knowledge, self-sufficiency (even though it may appear as arrogance), and perhaps even "goodness of heart and disinterestedness" (pp. 71–72). While Michels briefly suggests that democratic leaders may thus form a new aristocracy, the rule of the few but also the rule of the best, he turns shortly to the second pillar of the theory, the leaders' motivations, their practices, and the resulting tendency to autocracy.

EMPIRICAL OBSERVATIONS

Michels noted in respect to leaders a phenomenon that political scientists and citizens tend to notice even today, that once in office, leaders tend to stay there for long periods.

> *Certain individuals, simply for the reason that they have been invested with determinate functions, become irremovable, or at least difficult to replace. Every democratic organization rests, by its very nature, upon a division of labour. But whenever a division of labour prevails, there is necessarily specialization, and the specialists become indispensable (Michels, 1959, p. 101).*

In addition, Michels argues, leaders would not be willing to serve at all if they were "likely to be dismissed at any moment"; to justify their acquisition of complex skills, they must be assured of job stability (Michels, 1959, p. 102). The masses are grateful to leaders, even to the point of idolatry, Michels contends, and the masses fear chaos if the leaders are lost. The masses even acquiesce when leaders line their own pockets, since power and wealth "fascinate" the masses and stimulate the ambition "of all the more talented elements to enter the privileged bureaucracy of the labour movement" or beyond (p. 161). "The desire to dominate, for good or evil, is universal" and "every human power seeks to enlarge its prerogatives" (pp. 206-207).

Because leaders have, once in position, their own interests independent of the masses (although this is clothed in democratic rhetoric), and have many instruments at their command to manipulate the masses, most challenges to the leaders' positions come not from the masses but from contending elites, according to Michels. These challenges are opportunistic, he says, and occur when the incumbents show signs of weakness by failing to maintain touch with their supporters; or may be based on personality conflicts between "great men"; or on age-cohort differences, on differences in social background, or on regional stratification (Michels, 1959, p. 167). The result of such struggles should by now be predictable to Michels' readers: The conflicting parties do not defeat each other but instead accommodate one another, they "surrender a share of the spoil" to each other (p. 169).

EVALUATING THEORY

To the original question posed at the beginning of the chapter, What is a theory?, we now have one answer, Michels' iron law of oligarchy, which links specified variables (the division of labor, attitudes of masses and leaders, government outcomes) into a coherent, logically linked pattern of relations that explains some part of human activity. Beginning with democracy, Michels adds the incompetence of masses, as masses, to act; brings in delegation that creates representatives who become specialists in the public division of labor; shows that representatives develop their own interests independent of those of the masses, and these leaders are able to control the masses. Thus, democracy leads to oligarchy, and this happens in all cases. Notice you need not agree with it to accept that *it is a theory,* a connected set of propositions that say something definite about the real world.

Michels' iron law explains only certain phenomena, however. It does not explain (1) how people govern, whether well or ill; (2) what policies they put into effect; (3) which groups are favored or disfavored; (4) why leaders respond differently to similar problems; and so on. So having a universal theory does not imply you have a complete theory; there is always new work to be done.

IS THERE A USE FOR LARGE FUZZY THEORIES?

If Michels' iron law is one answer to the question, What is a theory?, there are other answers that take an entirely different approach. Among these is functional theory, which directs its attention not to specific individuals and their class-related organizational activities, but to the operation of social wholes as social wholes. The political science versions of functionalism, sometimes called structural-functionalism (Almond and Coleman, 1960), or sometimes not called functionalism at all, as in Easton's refusal to call his obviously functional systems theory by that name (1965) have now fallen on hard times. Both existed in the climate of the behavioral period, and except where incorporated in textbooks have both fallen out of favor as the behavioral movement fell out of favor, or perhaps more so.

Students of comparative politics should not, however, delude themselves that change in political science is linear, or that what is dead and buried today will not turn up again in the future, when everyone has grown tired of the currently stylish approaches and is looking for something that seems new and different. Indeed, where many political scientists think functionalism should be written off as a failed attempt to grasp political wholes such as societies and nations, other political scientists think functionalism is one of the best and brightest of theoretic hopes (Dogan and Pelassy, 1984). American political scientists especially, who are prone to accept only individualistic theories, for no better reason than that American culture trains us all in individualism as a social norm, need to learn to appreciate alternatives such as functionalism that throw events into a light entirely different from microanalytic theories.

Structural-functionalism as put forth by Almond and his several collaborators provides a place to reconsider functionalism, because it amply illustrated the major flaw in most "grand" functional theories. This flaw was their positive or optimistic bias, their assumption that social and political systems could be assumed to be carrying out all the functions or systemic necessities that were required to keep the system in good order. Thus the sociologist Parsons postulated functions such as "adaptation" and "pattern maintenance," which seemed to enshrine the status quo as the best of all worlds; and Almond and Coleman defined the political functions of rule making and execution, interest articulation and aggregation, which seemed to refer primarily to an optimally functioning, democratic, political system.

Easton's systems theory took a similar tack: Readers of Easton's systems trilogy find that he repeatedly acknowledges that individuals often behave in their own self-interest rather than in the system's interest, and that indeed leaders may be hazardous to the health of their followers; and yet he brushes these facts aside and allows theoretic access only to behavior that expresses the "public interest" or the needs of the whole system.[6] These strategies of thought led justly to criticisms that functionalism was conservative, concerned primarily with not rocking the social boat; idealistic, based on the most unrealistic and frequently indefinable assumptions, such as social equilibrium; and nontestable, not applicable to events in the real world. But are these faults inherent in the nature of functionalism or just in the work of the particular political scientists who have practiced it up to this time?

MIDDLE-RANGE FUNCTIONAL THEORY

There is an alternative functional tradition to which political scientists often refer but never seem actually to practice: that so-called "middle range" functional theory associated with the name of Robert Merton, a sociologist who took a quite different approach to functionalism than did Parsons. Merton's approach can be illustrated briefly by one of his best known studies, which inquired into the nature of the political machines and bossism so prevalent in American cities earlier in this century (Merton, 1957, pp. 71-82).

Where many political scientists of the period reacted to machines and political corruption in the cities by initiating or advocating reform movements, the use of professional city managers, and so on, Merton took a middle-level functional approach, asking why the machines existed, or, in other words, what function they served. His answer was that bosses and machine organizations served a social welfare function in times and places where there was no other source of such help. When a man was out of work he could go to the local machine representative and ask for, and probably get, either a job or something to tide the family over; when people got in trouble of various sorts, the machine had ways of untangling things; if people were too poor to celebrate holidays, the machine turned up with a turkey or children's toys. In return, of course, those who had been aided (or hoped to be) were expected to carry out the wishes of the organization when it called upon them. Functionalism of this sort puts city machines in a different light. The problem is not so much corruption but poverty and ignorance. You don't need a professional city manager so much as an improvement in economic conditions and education, because when these change, the machines naturally lose their hold.

THEORY AS A GUIDE TO INQUIRY

This version of functionalism is quite different from the "grand" sort of functionalism, and this middle-range functionalism is a fine and subtle instrument waiting to be put to good use by students of comparative politics. Instead of magisterially assuming that all working societies must, by definition, be fulfilling some highly abstract functional necessities, middle-range functionalism sets researchers thinking about the kinds of lower level functions that may be relevant to social behavior; about the kinds of people who may or may not fulfill the functions; and about what happens when no one fulfills the functions. For instance, what happens when the social welfare function (the need for help of poor and marginal individuals who are unable to survive on their own) is not met? One outcome is that the people in question starve—read Dickens on the disastrous conditions in the English slums of the nineteenth century. Generally, starving people do not rebel, so that is not a likely outcome, although one may wish to reconsult Scott and Popkin on the issue.

Another possible outcome of the failure of the welfare function is a deep, abiding discontent that creates a functional opportunity for someone to fan the discontent and achieve political prominence on the basis of fulfilling this unmet "functional necessity." This suggests that the functionalists were right about the existence of certain social needs that are larger than the needs of isolated individuals; insofar as groups of people in a society are in similar circumstances, and feel that something is not "right" about their lives, then a social need exists—there is a functional "necessity" ripe for exploitation.[7]

Middle-range functionalism is useful in directing attention beyond the actual observable operation of societies to their "invisible" aspects, the opportunities or dangers presented by certain configurations of events. A society in which there is excessive crime or violence offers opportunities for certain types of political behavior, and for politicians, in office or candidates for office, who advocate certain solutions. A large-scale comparative framework might be built on the type of functions different kinds of societies meet or fail to meet. By their problems, and their non-problems, societies might be compared almost independently of their actual government systems, except so far as those systems themselves create needs. Notice too that Michels' theory can be recast in middle-range functional terms.

THE POLITICAL ECONOMY APPROACH

There is a third major answer to the question, What is a theory?, that is different from either of the foregoing approaches, and this is rational choice theory, encountered earlier in the discussion of Downs and more recently with Popkin's peasants. Rational choice theory is frequently placed at the apex of the theoretic continuum, among those who practice this variety of theory, but it is preferable to see rational choice theory rather as one option among equals, for despite its admitted strengths, they come with such severe associated weaknesses that the theory, like all others, must be treated with skepticism and a willingness to substantially expand its premises.

Rational choice theory has never achieved in comparative politics anything like the popularity it has enjoyed among specialists in U.S. politics, or even among students of international relations. This difference is revealing of many of the problems of rational choice theory as a general theory of politics. It may be quite effective when it is possible to hold constant a whole variety of institutional and cultural variables. But when rational choice theory faces the wealth of variation found in the field of comparative politics, it quickly falls short.

In criticizing rational choice theory, however, one must be careful to remind oneself of its heroic role in the development of the political science discipline, a role that newcomers may overlook because they did not live through the behavioral revolution personally. If the "old" political science was swept aside during those years, rational choice theory was in the vanguard of the attacking forces, and was much more formidable than simple empiricism because it used all the weapons of theory, logic, and economic analysis. Why was it so destructive? It was destructive primarily because its approach undercut any sacredness that political institutions might have had for traditional thinkers, the ideas of democracy as an especially public philosophy, the belief in humankind's ability to construct for itself institutions that would be worthy of its higher nature.

THE ICONOCLASTIC FUNCTION

In the place of these hoary ideas, rational choice theorists such as Downs (1957), Simon (1965), Riker (1962) and Buchanan and Tullock (1962) put a model of man as individual, rational, greedy, and calculating; and the model applied to leaders and followers alike. The power of this idea was increased by its being presented with many of the most sophisticated tools of the economic profession, for the reputation of which political scientists have always had considerable reverence. But equally important was that rational choice theory so plainly predicted just the kind of behavior one could see by looking around at the existing practices of government and politicians. Men did wheel and deal, and public institutions often seemed to operate more for the private than the public good.

This said, however, the rational choice schools' originality was not maintained as new generations succeeded the founding fathers. Because so much of the credibility of rational choice theory depended upon its being an absolutely universal theory, more attention was devoted to ingenious efforts to prove its applicability to situations where it seemed inapplicable, than on the more sensible course of considering how the foundations of the theory might be enlarged beyond narrow economic behavior to wider issues of cognitive, intellectual, and norm-laden behavior. A recent suggestion of how this goal might be achieved is Aaron Wildavsky's suggestion of a "cultural" rationality, which allows an expansion of human goals beyond monetary self-interest to a far wider range of culturally conditioned goals such as duty, service, salvation, or power (Wildavsky, 1987). This is an old idea, tracing back at least in modern political science to the work of Harold Lasswell (Lasswell and Kaplan, 1950), but it has never previously been incorporated into empirical research models. The modification is especially relevant to students of comparative politics because it builds into the deductive base of rational theory a model of variant idea systems on which choice can be based, thus combining logical rigor with a wider appreciation of the many goals—ethical, idealistic, or social, as well as economic—upon which people act in their political lives.[8]

THE CULTURAL RATIONALITY MODEL

Comparative politics is not without resources to meet Wildavsky's suggestion, and the source of these resources illustrates why political scientists may profit from reading the works of their predecessors. A book about political culture, published as long ago as 1965, contained a series of studies on various countries in the developing world that encapsulated their operating principles in a manner fully appropriate to insertion in a rational decision model (Pye and Verba, 1965). Decision rules for members of Turkish village society as suggested by the analysis of Dankwart Rustow, might, for instance, be formalized as follows (Pye and Verba, 1965, pp. 171–198; Lane, 1992).

> *1. The group's welfare is more important than the individual's.*
> *2. But where there is no conflict, the individual is free to act on his own (to pursue personal wealth, for instance).*
> *3. The group is a hierarchy based upon age (which measures "wisdom" or experience).*
> *4. The group's welfare is defined by the elders; and therefore their directions are to be loyally obeyed.*
> *5. These directions typically include:*
>
> > *a. Islamic austerity*
> > *b. Courage in protecting the group (martial bravery, stoicism, etc.)*

While ordinary people will not of course work out their beliefs with such formality, this cultural idea system serves to make explicit the foundations upon which village behavior seems to proceed. Although it defines a pattern of behavior and not a conscious logic, the belief model is obvious, simple, and with minor modifications applicable to many similar societies or groups.

Leonard Binder's description of middle-class Egyptian political culture describes another "rational" choice model, and shows how a norm system can be both "traditional" and "modern" (Pye and Verba, 1965, pp. 396-449).

> *1. If in a superior position, the individual is required to "pay off" his followers through beneficial policies, and other goods; and is entitled to expect, from those followers, deference and respect.*
> *2. When in a subordinate role, the individual is expected to be loyal, deferent, self-sacrificing.*

3. Where the hierarchical roles are inapplicable, the individual is expected to behave competitively (Lane, 1992, p. 371)

Since this model is taken from rural Egypt, it is curious to note how similar it is to the bureaucratic model developed, for instance, by Gordon Tullock (1965) and others.

These examples, with their diversity of belief, of logic, of strategy, and of policy, vividly illustrate how narrow is the self-interest axiom of the rational choice theorists, but also how easy it is to open it out to include widely diverse attitudes. All are, in a sense, self-interested, but the manifestations are so sweepingly unlike simple economic rationality, and so unlike each other, that the cultural model's necessity and its vitality become clear.

METHODS OF THEORY BUILDING

A constant theme throughout this discussion of the recent history of the field of comparative politics has been the centrality of theory in political research. Behavioralism was a leap into an unknown future where theory would preside; development research proceeded under the field's first attempts at theory; the statists revived old European theories in the hope of making their ideas useful for comparative politics; and state-society theory and the new institutional theories have adopted yet other theoretic interests. But this brief review reveals why nothing definitive has yet been said, in the present essay, about the nature of theory.

The reason for this reticence is that theory has, over recent decades, changed its meaning more than once. To retain a belief that there is one "best" type of theory is to ignore the diversity of the theoretic enterprise. That reality—the multiplicity of types of theory—is a major reason for the title's being the "art" of comparative politics. There are of course rules for theory building, but the rules are in themselves inadequate for comparative research because they are incomplete. Science must therefore proceed with the assistance of art—open-minded creativity in working with the materials that make up the field in which one has chosen to work. Those who do research in the physical sciences have always known this; social scientists are beginning to catch on.

The do-it-yourself nature of the sciences is the argument made in one of the classic works in social science theory, Lave and March's *Introduction to Models in the Social Sciences* (1975). Since the lesson is one that many comparativists have learned on their own but have never paused to articulate, it is helpful to use this work of methodology to clarify some of the fundamental techniques involved in building theory or models (the authors use the terms interchangeably). Lave and March emphasize a way of looking at the world that is innovative. Instead of asking the scientist to collect reams of data and allowing the computer to do the analysis, Lave and March advocate an almost quaintly old-fashioned approach to inquiry—thinking about facts, in a common-sense, probing, intelligent way. The basic rule that guides inquiry, according to these authors, is to start with a known fact, often a perplexing fact, and to ask one-self "how it might have come about." The answers to this question become the hypotheses of the model or theory, and can then be tested against observed reality.

"'DUMB" THEORIZING

Lave and March delight in the invention of close-to-home, simple examples of how the theory-building process works, in order to puncture the common notion that "theory" is an esoteric exercise suitable only to geniuses. As an example of this approach, take their case of the "dumb" athletes; or, to put it more politely, the question of why it is in school situations that persons active in athletics are so often stereotyped as less academically acute than their nonathletic schoolmates.

The question with which Lave and March begin is not "Why are athletes dumb?" but (and this is a major shift in the style of inquiry) why are they "perceived" to be so? Of course, this is quite a different matter, and it forces the inquirer to use his or her head in an active, positive, imaginative way. Lave and March's suggested theories for this small but not uninteresting case are easy enough—one might easily have thought them up oneself, had one put one's mind to it. First, athletes' academic weakness may simply be a result of lack of time; they spend so many hours on the track or field, or in the gym, that they do not have time left for study. To test such a theory the inquiring theorist need merely observe athletes in their off season and see whether their performance goes up.

But one theory alone will not do the job, so the authors explore further possibilities, such as that human beings generally need to excel in only one field in order to maintain their self-esteem, and athletes—being satisfied in their athletic work that provides esteem—do not bother to seek further glories. Another theory proposed by Lave and March, and one that demonstrates a truly scientific objectivity, is that athletes are not dumb at all but that their peers are jealous of their success and systematically denigrate their intelligence even when they do well in schoolwork (Lave and March, 1975, pp. 58-60). Thus, Lave and March illustrate in simple cases that theory is not mystical but practical. This is a vital lesson, and one that comparativists have learned, in their own way, over recent decades.

Lave and March describe several characteristics of this pattern of theory-construction that help to clarify what such theory entails. They emphasize first the study of "processes" underlying observable events; second, the use of "implications" as a dynamic way of tying together sequences of facts; third, the effort to generalize so that one's conclusions are carefully raised to higher levels of scientific significance; and finally, "explanation" as the criterion of good theory (Lave and March, 1975, pp. 40–42). Examples from recent comparative politics research put flesh on these theoretic bones.

Attention to underlying processes, Lave and March's first point, is characteristic of Barrington Moore's analysis of democracy, fascism, and communism, where his interest is centered almost wholly not on the governmental forms but on the underlying forces that produced them. "Process" means the identification of the basic relevant actors in the field of study (aristocracy, peasants, bourgeoisie), and the delineation of how they interacted, each according to its own resources, goals, and circumstances, to create the different government outcomes.

THE LOGIC OF IMPLICATIONS

Lave and March's second point—the use of implications in order to build a rounded model of a political process—is especially evident in Huntington's (1968) analysis of the development process, because Huntington "fills in" the matrix of known facts by providing general connectors that show the political logic of various situations, a logic that is not always directly observable. In modeling the predicament of a king forced to pursue development policies lest his competitors make backwardness an issue, Huntington credits him with a least some ability to peer into the future, making specific implications from known regularities of political life. "The bourgeoisie is with me today because they are hungry for economic opportunity, but when they get richer and more powerful they will become my worst enemies."

Lave and March show how strong such a theoretical approach can be, despite its differences with simple empiricism which only collects facts and would think it presumptuous to go "beyond" those immediately observable facts. Familiarity with the comparativists discussed in earlier chapters shows, however, how dynamic implications can reveal underlying causes and enrich inquiry.

The issue of generalizability, Lave and March's third point, is essential to science, which seeks to discover "universal" facts. Positivism, the philosophy of science that was adopted by the behavioralists in political science, argued that there was only one way to achieve universality: by discovering propositions of the form "All x are y," and not allowing any qualifying adjectives to weaken the force of the "all." It was not considered proper, for instance, to say that economically motivated persons would do x, and politically motivated persons would do y, and so on. The qualifying adjectival phrases made such statements equivalent to saying all persons are mortal except sometimes they are not, according to this viewpoint.

Generalizability takes on a new meaning in Lave and March's model-building approach. Instead of collecting variables into grand statistical summaries, the new approach carves its way into the center of political processes and shows that, underlying the different surface facts, a single core process is involved. It is this identification of a core *political process* that makes comparative models universal. A fine example of this pattern is Migdal's (1988) "survival" theory, which begins with observations on peasant villagers who must adapt their life strategies to the exigencies around them: physical exigencies such as land, climate and crops; and social exigencies such as the need to placate the local strongman, whose assistance they may need when something goes awry—bad harvests, trouble with the law, illness.

But Migdal's theory does not stop with this first level, it rises to notice that strongmen also have their problems of survival (rebellions clients, insufficient resources); as do local officials (rebellions strongmen, bureaucratic superiors), and so on up to the top of the political pile where presidents and other high politicians also struggle for survival against their own particular odds. In this way, clarification of a "process" at one level may be generalized to many levels, and may create a model with wide-ranging applicability.

FIND YOURSELF AN EIGHT-YEAR-OLD

What is a "good theory"? For Lave and March it is "all of the above" plus one final defining characteristic, the quality of explanation. Explanation is obviously necessary, but is slightly ambiguous as a criterion because different people may find different explanations appropriate, depending on their level of information and background knowledge, and on their purposes. One workable solution to this problem is to specify to whom explanations should be directed; and one plausible audience may be defined as bright eight-year-old kids. People who use this criterion argue that children of this age are sufficiently grown up that they are curious and critical—they are, in fact, the ones who notice when emperors have no clothes—and they are good natural judges of what "makes sense." Older children, according to this argument, have already begun to take on the quality of adults, and have a tendency to be satisfied with conventional theories, or to be impressed by empty and pretentious ones.

Whatever audience one chooses, "explanation" involves presenting all the major elements in a political process, showing how they interact to produce observed outcomes, and how these outcomes restructure the future interactive situation by the rules and resources and sometimes even the participants. As this makes plain, the explanatory emphasis lies in the logic of the causal connections. The older method of evaluating theory was its ability merely to predict, and this hardly expanded one's knowledge. Prediction would have been content to say that if you slept overnight in the marshes you would catch malaria. This might have been sufficient for the health-conscious, but not for science, which was only satisfied when it identified the mosquito's role in carrying the plasmodium that caused the disease.

EPILOGUE

What then is theory? Or, more specifically, what is theory in comparative politics? It is a quest, as the history here recounted has shown. But it is not a fruitless quest: Some conclusions have been reached. Comparativists have, over a couple score of years, reached an opening in the woods, where the visibility is better than it is in the deepest parts of the forest. In this "clearing" comparativists find themselves increasingly uncomfortable with whole-system generalizing that cannot be analyzed operationally into concrete individuals or unified groups. "Progress" or "development" or "democracy" are no longer seen as forces working themselves out in the everyday world.

Activity instead is sited in individual human beings who may act to bring about progress or democracy, if they define their goals as being forwarded by such behavior; but individuals also who may not be useful to the system. Many tyrants prefer their people to live in poverty, ignorance, and fear. Even popular democratic politicians may prefer that their activities not be too transparently clear to the people they govern. The state-society perspective on political systems has brought comparative politics to this realistic appraisal of political behavior, and it will be difficult to retreat from such an obviously practical viewpoint.

To summarize the argument of this review of comparative history, it is useful to bring together the elements of this model that various comparativists, working on their own but within the larger context of the comparative field, have over the years hammered into shape. The answer might be left as an exercise, to be "read off" from earlier chapters that showed that a "politics" model kept turning up as a way of providing deep political explanations for a variety of individual problems and topics. But the model is compact and easy to summarize—as models indeed should be—and it serves as a conclusion to the present analysis.

The politics model defines individual actors as engaged in a dynamic process within institutions that their behavior serves to reinforce, to modify, or to overthrow. This political process centers on the practical confrontation of individual persons as they debate or negotiate issues that involve not only the distribution of the goods and evils of life, but of the rules controlling both distribution and overall governance. The key to this political confrontation lies in the type and amount of resources the participants can call upon; one recalls here Huntington's memorable phrase about the rich using bribery, the students using riots, and the military using coups (1968).

Political struggles are not always as clearly observable as one might expect. In many societies the politics seems silent and there appears to be perfect tranquility—until someone imposes the straw that breaks some camel's back, and the peace is shattered. Only depth analysis can recognize the possibilities inherent in some situation before they actually rise to the surface.

When the comparativist goes forth into the field, to study some country, town, village, organization, some group of any kind, does the comparative politics model provide research guidance? Study of those who have practiced it suggests that the model does provide guidance.

- The first step is to determine who are the major participants, those who are actively engaged in, or appear as if they may come to engage in, the business of the group. These activists are distinguished from the "audience" in order to simplify the analysis, but it is remembered that audiences may, if conditions change, break into the action arena.
- For all participants must be defined the idea systems, the beliefs, attitudes, goals, and values that structure their view of the world and their purposes in entering

the arena. Important here are both individual ideas and group ideas, the latter studied under the heading of political culture.

- The next step is the discovery of the "rules," both explicit and implicit, under which the group operates. Who has the right to take what kinds of actions—who pays, who spends, who obeys, who rules? And, of course, who disdains following rules?
- The realistic estimation of the participants' resources is the next step. Resources here include not only physical resources but the ideas that may give some members precedence over others; the allies that may be called upon; the numbers of persons in some affected groups; and even obstinacy, the triumph of will over mere facts.
- The nature of the interaction in any comparative politics model will depend on the underlying structure of the situation, which defines what the opportunities and constraints on behavior will be, on the basis of the types of participants, their number, their resources, and their ideas. A field in which all actors are equally endowed, both cognitively and physically, will lead to equitable, light government. A field in which one man is aggressive and ninety-nine others are timid will surely become an autocracy.
- The structure of the situation will, next, create certain functional opportunities, physical and social realities that qualify as needs to be met and invite members or outsiders to fulfill them. Thus a famine creates a need for food for the starving, and a political opportunity to those who provide it. Or an incompetent leader creates a functional opportunity for a coup.

The beauty of the politics model as practiced by many of the comparative theorists discussed in the course of this essay is the logical structure within which these elements are combined. One comes across the pattern again and again in the works of Huntington, Migdal, Wallerstein, Moore, Skocpol, Evans, Scott and Popkin: *Because* of a given situation (inadequate room for national expansion, or a weak bourgeoisie, or oversized turbulent urban populations, or sandy soil), *then* a certain situation arose, which changed the political situations of the participants, so that a new situation ensued and so on until one reaches the conclusion that this interlocked set of processes has provided an *explanation*.

It is a simple model, and it works. That has been the moral of our tale.

NOTES

1. Ball (1987) has made this point forcefully in his discussion of the relation between the philosophy of science and political science. He suggests that political scientists must become less dogmatic about falsifying theories, and more charitable in evaluating them (pp. 34–35).

2. Dahl as well as Michels has strong social democratic sympathies (Baer, Jewell, and Sigelman, 1991). Note that Dahl's refutation of a single coherent elite does not really meet Michels' argument, since Michels never said there was such a unified elite, only elites.

3. Stinchcombe (1968) provides an excellent discussion of the several levels of theoretical construction.

4. The issue is a complex one. Students should begin with Hempel (1965) and Popper (1959); and can bring themselves into the current level of discussion with Giere (1988).

5. See the discussion in Chapters 2 and 4 above.

6. Easton raises the issue of nonresponse by elites late in his discussion of the systems approach, and admits that authorities may seek to pursue their own purposes even against the objectives of other members. But he concludes: "we do not have to pursue this line of discussion further" (1965a, p. 44l). This refusal to look at negative systems is perplexing in a theorist who sought to build a general theory.

7. Terry Moe touches on these issues in his organization theory, which emphasizes the role of entrepreneurs who invent new interest groups in areas where old interest groups fail to cover issues relevant to some sectors of the public (1980).

8. See Lane (1992) for a fuller discussion of cultural rationality.

REFERENCES

Almond, Gabriel A., and James S. Coleman (Eds.). *The Politics of the Developing Areas*. Princeton: Princeton University Press, 1960.

Baer, Michael A., Malcolm E. Jewell, and Lee Sigelman (Eds.). *Political Science in America: Oral Histories of a Discipline*. Lexington: University of Kentucky, 1991.

Ball, Terence. (Ed.) *Idioms of Inquiry: Critique and Renewal in Political Science*. Albany: SUNY Press, 1987.

Buchanan, James M. and Gordon Tullock. *The Calculus of Consent* (1962). Ann Arbor: University of Michigan Press, 1965.

Dahl, Robert A. *Who Governs?* New Haven: Yale University Press, 1961.

Dogan, Mattei, and Dominique Pelassy. *How to Compare Nations: Strategies in Comparative Politics*. Chatham: Chatham House, 1984.

Downs, Anthony. *An Economic Theory of Democracy*. New York: Harper and Row, 1957.

Easton, David. *The Political System: An Inquiry into the State of Political Science*. New York: Alfred A. Knopf, 1953.

Easton, David. *A Framework for Political Analysis*. Englewood Cliffs: Prentice Hall, 1965a.

Easton, David. *A Systems Analysis of Political Life*. New York: John Wiley and Sons, 1965b.

Giere, Ronald N. *Explaining Science: A Cognitive Approach*. Chicago: University of Chicago Press, 1988.

Hempel, Carl Gustav. *Aspects of Scientific Explanation: And Other Essays in the Philosophy of Science*. New York: The Free Press, 1965.

Huntington, Samuel P. *Political Order in Changing Societies*. New Haven: Yale University Press, 1968.

Lane, Ruth. "Political Culture: Residual Category or General Theory?" *Comparative Political Studies* 25, no. 3 (October 1992): 362–87.

Lasswell, Harold D., and Abraham Kaplan. *Power and Society: A Framework for Political Inquiry*. New Haven: Yale University Press, 1950.

Lave, Charles, and James March. *An Introduction to Models in the Social Sciences*. New York: Harper & Row, 1975.

Merton, Robert K. *Social Theory and Social Structure* (Revised and Enlarged Edition, 1957). New York: The Free Press, 1949.

Michels, Robert. *Political Parties: A Sociological Study of the Oligarchical Tendencies of Modern Democracy* (1915). New York: Dover, 1959.

Migdal, Joel S. *Strong Societies and Weak States: State-Society Relations and State Capabilities in the Third World*. Princeton: Princeton University Press, 1988.

Moe, Terry. *The Organization of Interests: Incentives and Internal Dynamics of Political Interest Groups*. Chicago: University of Chicago Press, 1980.

Parsons, Talcott. *The Social System*. Glencoe: Free Press, 1951.

Popper, Karl R. *The Logic of Scientific Discovery* (1935). New York: Harper Torchbooks, 1959.

Pye, Lucien W., and Sidney Verba (Eds.). *Political Culture and Political Development*. Princeton: Princeton University Press, 1965.

Riker, William H. *The Theory of Political Coalitions*. New Haven: Yale University Press, 1962.

Simon, Herbert A. *Administrative Behavior: A Study of Decision-Making Process in Administrative Organization* (1945). New York: Free Press, 1965.

Stinchcombe, Arthur L. *Constructing Social Theories*. New York: Harcourt, Brace, World, 1968.

Tullock, Gordon. *The Politics of Bureaucracy*. Washington: Public Affairs Press, 1965.

Wildavsky, Aaron. "Choosing Preferences by Constructing Institutions: A Cultural Theory of Preference Formation." *American Political Science Review* LXXXI, no. 1 (March 1987): 3–21.

Index